Chicago and New York: Architectural Interactions

The Art Institute of Chicago 1984

This catalogue is published in connection with the exhibition "Chicago and New York: More Than a Century of Architectural Interaction," co-organized by The Art Institute of Chicago and The New-York Historical Society and presented at the following institutions:

The Art Institute of Chicago
March 8—July 29, 1984

The American Institute of Architects Foundation, the Octagon, Washington, D.C.
October 17, 1984—January 6, 1985

Farish Gallery, Rice University, Houston
February 11—March 31, 1985

The New-York Historical Society
May 22—October 26, 1985

Both this catalogue and the exhibition it accompanies were supported by grants from the National Endowment for the Arts and the Graham Foundation for Advanced Studies in the Fine Arts.

© 1984 by The Art Institute of Chicago. All rights reserved. Printed in the United States of America.

Library of Congress Catalog Card Number 83-073268
ISBN 0-86559-056-7

Designed by Michael Glass Design, Chicago
Typeset by Harlan Typographic, Dayton
Printed by Rohner Printing Company, Chicago

Cover: D. H. Burnham and Co., Architects. Perspective Rendering of the Flatiron Building, New York, 1902, delineated by Jules Guérin. (cat. 4)

Contents

Foreword — 4
James N. Wood and James B. Bell

Acknowledgments — 5
John Zukowsky

Color plates — 6

The Capitals of American Architecture: Chicago and New York — 12
John Zukowsky

The Nineteenth Century: The Projecting of Chicago as a Commercial City and the Rationalization of Design and Construction — 30
David Van Zanten

Sister Cities: Architecture and Planning in the Twentieth Century — 50
Carol Herselle Krinsky

Commentaries on Chicago and New York — 77

Catalogue — 85

Foreword

Chicago and New York have consistently vied with each other to be the capital of American architecture. This catalogue, along with the exhibition it accompanies, tells some of that story and relates as well the important interchange that has taken place between these two great cities. It also gives us the opportunity to see some of the architectural treasures at two institutions that have long been witness to this interaction and, occasionally, its intercity rivalry: The New-York Historical Society and The Art Institute of Chicago. Both institutions house massive collections, including a wealth of architectural drawings, photographs, and archival records that are essential for historians to document accurately the competitive growth of Chicago and New York and the contributions that their architects have made to the American cityscape. Both institutions owe much of the development of their architectural collections to the generosity of architects. Here in Chicago, it was the bequest of architect and planner Daniel H. Burnham in 1912 that established an architectural library at the Art Institute. Furthermore, Burnham's mentor, the New York architect Peter Bonnett Wight, who established his practice in Chicago following the fire of 1871, was the first to donate a set of architectural drawings to the museum in 1919.

The Art Institute of Chicago is pleased to cosponsor this exhibition, "Chicago and New York: More Than a Century of Architectural Interaction," with The New-York Historical Society. I wish to express our gratitude for the support of the National Endowment for the Arts and the Graham Foundation for Advanced Studies in the Fine Arts, whose contributions helped make possible this volume and the exhibition it accompanies.

James N. Wood, Director
The Art Institute of Chicago

It is a pleasure for The New-York Historical Society to participate in this cooperative project with The Art Institute of Chicago. Since acquiring a set of architectural drawings by John McComb, Jr., in the 1880s, The New-York Historical Society has developed a wide-ranging collection of architectural materials. From renderings and blueprints to business records and correspondence, this collection documents a fascinating story of personal creativity in the growing metropolis. On the forge of social and economic change we see perennial needs met through new forms and structures. The experience is common to New York and Chicago, and in these cities has issued in equally striking expressions of the architectural imagination. As this exhibition shows, interaction coexisted with contrast; and, from suburb to skyscraper, the comparative picture suggests new areas of research in architectural and urban history. I look forward to the pursuit of such scholarship, and to the continued cooperation among institutions that is necessary for its development and display.

James B. Bell, Director
The New-York Historical Society

Acknowledgments

The idea for an exhibition on the architectural interactions between Chicago and New York first occurred to me in 1978, soon after I had moved from New York to Chicago to begin work at The Art Institute of Chicago. In many ways the inspiration came from the Paris-New York, Paris-Berlin, and Paris-Moscow exhibitions that were organized by the Centre George Pompidou in the late 1970s. In 1983 support from the National Endowment for the Arts and the Graham Foundation for Advanced Studies in the Fine Arts made possible the organization of this exhibition in conjunction with The New-York Historical Society. In addition, a very generous gift from the Thomas J. and Mary E. Eyerman Foundation enabled the Art Institute to purchase specifically for inclusion in this show the important rendering by Jules Guérin of New York's famed Flatiron Building (cat. 4) designed by Chicago's Daniel H. Burnham.

In order to implement this exhibition and to produce its catalogue, a number of other people assisted us, and they are greatly to be thanked for their participation. First of all, the Art Institute's Committee on Architecture—David C. Hilliard (Chairman), James N. Alexander, Edwin J. De Costa, Stanley M. Freehling, Bruce J. Graham, Neil Harris, Carter H. Manny, Jr., Mrs. J. A. Pritzker, Stuart Scott, Charles H. Shaw, and Stanley Tigerman—was enthusiastically supportive of this project. Second, the cocurators of the exhibition, Mosette Glaser Broderick, Carol Herselle Krinsky, and David Van Zanten, were especially cooperative in defining the nature of the exhibition and in selecting objects to be included. Third, within both the Art Institute and The New-York Historical Society are many staff members who deserve a special thanks. At the Art Institute: Pauline Saliga, the Assistant Curator of Architecture; Daphne C. Roloff and Susan Godlewski of the Ryerson and Burnham Libraries; Robert V. Sharp, who edited the exhibition catalogue, and Susan F. Rossen, of the Publications Department; Conservator Timothy Lennon; Registrar Wallace Bradway; Celia Marriott, Associate Director of Media Programming, and Lou Mallozzi, Audio-Visual Producer; Museum Photographer John Mahtesian; and Reynold Bailey, Coordinator of Art Installation. At The New-York Historical Society: Elizabeth Mize Currie, Coordinator of Exhibitions; Mary Alice Kennedy, Registrar; Wendy Shadwell, Curator of Prints; Carole A. Slatkin, Assistant Director for Public Programs; Larry Sullivan, Librarian; and Helena Zinkham, Curator of Prints. I should also like to thank two former staff members of The New-York Historical Society, Mary Black and Edith Sakell, who were supportive of the project in its very early stages.

A number of people outside these institutions generously contributed their ideas, time, and assistance. Among them are the architects, critics, and historians who were willing to provide their opinions on the essence of the Chicago-New York interaction. Many others assisted as volunteers on various tasks related to the exhibition and its catalogue—securing photographs, tracking down historical information, or suggesting and locating objects for the exhibition: Tisha Bauer, Robert Bruegmann, Rita Caviglia, Sally Chappell, Clare Gearty, Janet Ginsburg, Christopher Gray, John Gronkowski, Emily Harris, Susan Harris, Bob Hashimoto, John Hill, Julie Iovine, Sharon Irish, Peggy Knox, Charles Landefeld, Jonathan Miller, Luigi Mumford, Rita Muncie, Keith Palmer, Milli Payton, David Phillips, Charles Ward Rapp, Richard Staub, Erica Stoller, Bob Thall, Joseph Tichenor, Charles Tint, John Vinci, C. William Westfall, Guy Whitney, and Mary Woolever. Rick Tickner restored the Gilbert Elevated Railroad model on exhibit (cat. 9), while Bob Weinberg of Graphic Conservation and Mel Theobald conserved a number of the drawings shown. I wish to thank the staff of the David and Alfred Smart Gallery of the University of Chicago—Reinhold Heller, Acting Director; Richard Born, Curator; Mary Braun, Registrar—for allowing Mel Theobald to use their conservation facilities. I also wish to acknowledge the assistance of Fannia Weingartner in the preparation of exhibition labels and didactic materials. I am exceedingly grateful both to Susan Johnson of Graphics Group for her elegant design of the exhibition's graphics and installation and to Michael Glass for the splendid design of this catalogue. Robert Bruegmann prepared the script for the slide tape show, and architectural artist James Smith prepared a special mural for the projection booth based on the Chicago-New York theme of this show. Finally, for their help with the traveling of this exhibition I wish to thank Drexel Turner of the Farish Gallery of Rice University in Houston and Susan Stein of the Octagon of the American Institute of Architects Foundation in Washington, D.C.

John Zukowsky
Curator of Architecture
The Art Institute of Chicago

Plate 1, see cat. 12

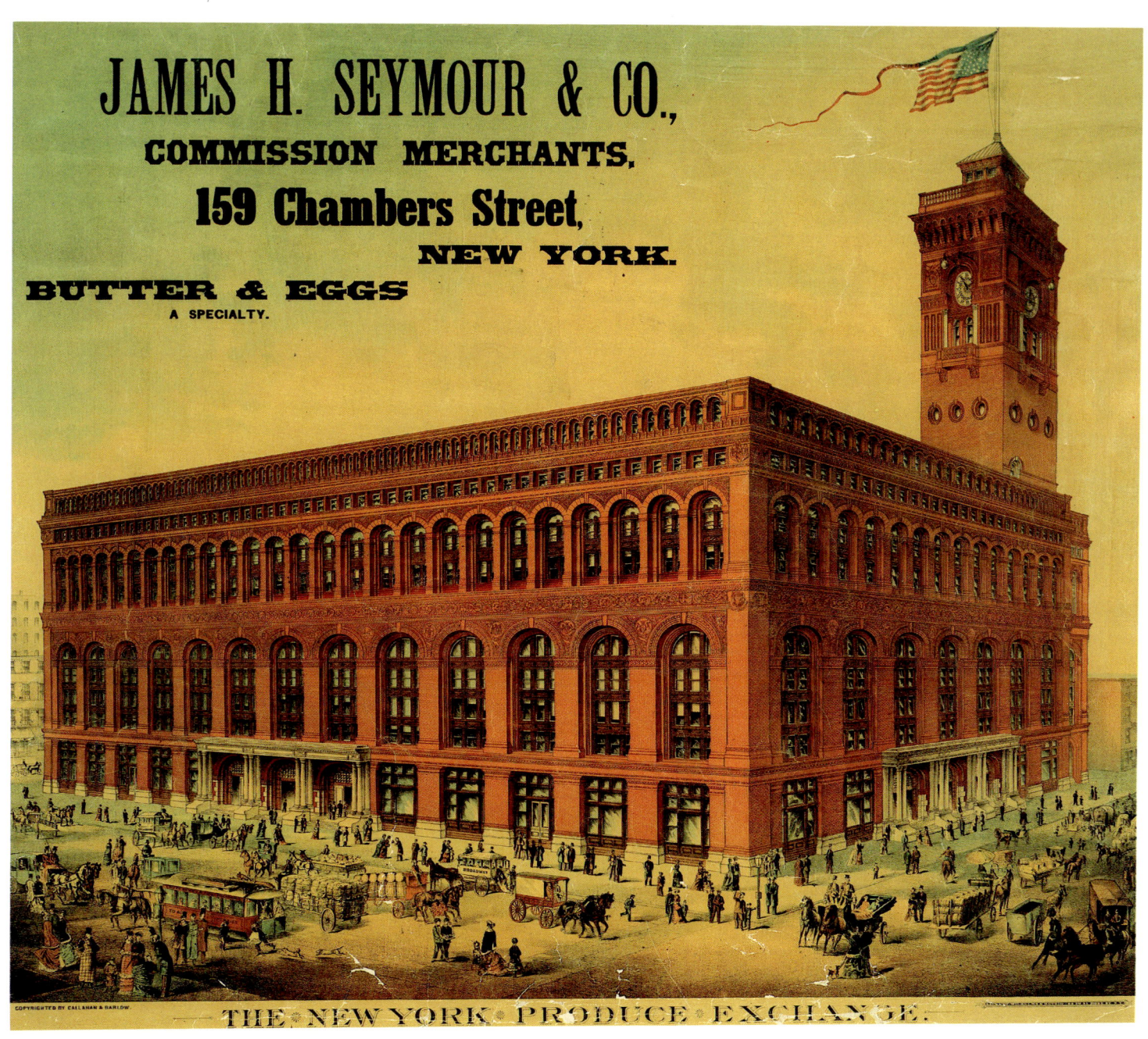

Plate 2, see cat. 48

Plate 3, see cat. 51

Plate 4, see cat. 55

Plate 5, see cat. 57

Plate 6, see cat. 75

The Capitals of American Architecture: Chicago and New York

John Zukowsky

Chicago and New York—these are often thought to be the two great superpowers of American architecture. Architects consider each city to have its own style, its own way of shaping its local environment, its own individualistic contributions to the history of architecture. Yet these contributions were not developed in isolation. Throughout the 19th and 20th centuries there has been, and still is, a considerable amount of competitive interaction between architects, contractors, and developers in both cities.

This exhibition and catalogue draw upon existing histories of the architecture of both cities and add new ideas to them, but no single effort can contain a complete account of all the interactions between Chicago and New York. Carl Condit has written several architectural histories of Chicago, and he and Sarah Bradford Landau are currently at work on a book about New York's skyscrapers. Gerald Larson is preparing a multivolume counterpart on the Chicago skyscraper. Robert A. M. Stern's *New York 1900* was released while this catalogue was in press. Robert Bruegmann's research on the skyscraper will supplement earlier publications on that subject by Paul Goldberger and Ada Louise Huxtable. Andrew Alpern has published a survey of New York apartments, and comparable projects on Chicago apartments are being done by Wim de Wit and C. William Westfall.[1] In short, these and other publications now underway will provide an enormous body of knowledge about Chicago, New York, and their architectural interaction. The multiplicity of viewpoints expressed in this exhibition, the following catalogue essays, and commentaries by selected architects, critics, and historians offer additional observations on the architectural relationships between these two cities and stimulate thought about future interchanges.

At the simplest level of interactions, Chicago architects have designed New York projects and New Yorkers Chicago ones. In this exhibition, works by Peter Bonnett Wight, James Renwick, McKim, Mead and White, and Daniel Burnham (see cats. 1-4) attest to this exchange. Other examples from the past include the Parfitt Brothers' Tree Studios Building (fig. 1), Louis Sullivan's Bayard-Condict Building of 1897-98 (fig. 2), David Adler's townhouse for Mrs. Evelyn Field (fig. 3), the 1927 Paramount Building by Rapp and Rapp (fig. 4), Ludwig Mies van der Rohe's fa-

Fig. 1 Parfitt Brothers, Architects, with Hill and Woltersdorf, Associate Architects. Tree Studios Building, State Street, between Ohio and Ontario Streets, Chicago. 1894.

Fig. 2 Louis H. Sullivan, Architect, with Lyndon P. Smith, Associate Architect. Bayard-Condict Building, 65-69 Bleecker Street, New York. 1897-98.

Fig. 3 David Adler, Architect, with Robert Work, Associate Architect. Field Residence, 4-8 East 70th Street, New York. 1925-27 (now demolished).

Fig. 4 Rapp and Rapp, Architects. Paramount Building, Broadway and 43rd Street, New York. 1927 (later altered).

mous Seagram Tower of 1955-57, designed with Philip Johnson (fig. 5), and Edward Durell Stone's Standard Oil Building of 1970 (fig. 6). Two recent examples can also be cited. The New York firm of Kohn, Pedersen and Fox has completed an office building at 333 West Wacker Drive in Chicago (fig. 7), and the Chicago office of Skidmore, Owings and Merrill designed the 875 Third Avenue Building in New York. This elementary exchange will certainly continue in the future. John Burgee with Philip Johnson has designed a skyscraper for 190 South La Salle Street, Kohn, Pedersen and Fox is planning one for 900 North Michigan Avenue (fig. 8), while Helmut Jahn of Murphy/Jahn is planning Park Avenue Tower and 425 Lexington Avenue (cats. 5, 65). Sometimes, the results of this interaction are more complex, involving transposed imagery or more complicated stylistic influences. I shall briefly explore four Chicago examples of complex interactions.

The first of these is the Bryan Lathrop House (1892) by Charles F. McKim of McKim, Mead and White of New York. Its bow-front, Georgian style facade (fig. 9) recalls eastern townhouse architecture, particularly because the architect paid close attention to the design of the main facade as part of an urban streetscape, as with New York row houses (see cats. 21, 22). The design departs from the Chicago townhouse solution, which is more like a freestanding suburban house with several facades ornamented, as in Adler and Sullivan's Straus House (cat. 23), Richard Schmidt's Madlener House of 1902 (cat. 30), or even Stanford White's Patterson House (cat. 3).[2] Although some Fifth Avenue and Riverside Drive mansions from turn-of-the-century New York were also designed as freestanding suburban houses, they were usually on a much greater scale and more elaborately ornamented than Chicago chateaux and urban villas (see cats. 24-26). Holabird and Roche were the associate architects for the Lathrop House, and they have traditionally been credited with supervising the construction of the New Yorkers' design. Yet the complete set of drawings for the house in the Art Institute and the Chicago Historical Society indicates that the Chicago firm was actively involved with designing and redesigning the classical interiors of the building through the 1890s, in a continuation of an architect-client relationship established a decade earlier with the Lathrop family.

In contrast with the considerable contribution to design by Holabird and Roche throughout the Lathrop house, the associate architects Fugard and Knapp probably had little influence on the design of the Allerton House (1924) by Murgatroyd and Ogden. Allerton Houses were a New York chain of "club-hotels"—residential hotels for single men and

THE CAPITALS OF AMERICAN ARCHITECTURE

Fig. 5 Ludwig Mies van der Rohe, Architect, with Philip Johnson, Associate Architect. Seagram Building, 375 Park Avenue, New York. 1954-58.

Fig. 6 Edward Durell Stone, Architect, with Perkins and Will, Associate Architects. Standard Oil Building, 200 East Randolph Street, Chicago. 1970.

Fig. 7 William Pedersen of Kohn, Pedersen and Fox, Architects, with Perkins and Will, Associate Architects. 333 West Wacker Drive, Chicago. 1981-83.

Fig. 8 William Pedersen of Kohn, Pedersen and Fox, Architects. Model of Preliminary Design for 900 North Michigan Avenue, Chicago. 1983.

THE CAPITALS OF AMERICAN ARCHITECTURE

Fig. 9 McKim, Mead and White, Architects, with Holabird and Roche, Associate Architects. Bryan Lathrop House, 120 East Bellevue Place, Chicago. 1892.

women. The Allerton House on Michigan Avenue (fig. 10), the chain's first building outside New York, was an emissary of a New York image. Murgatroyd and Ogden specialized in designing comparably detailed hotels such as the Governor Clinton and the Barbizon in New York. The brick Italian Romanesque style and massing of Allerton House is more akin to Park Avenue hotels and apartment houses of the 1920s than, for example, to Fugard and Knapp's Georgian and Renaissance apartment buildings in Chicago, such as 60-70 East Scott Street (1917), 229 East Lake Shore Drive (1918), 220-22 East Walton Place (1919-20), and 219 East Lake Shore Drive (1922). These differences indicate that Fugard and Knapp probably provided supervisory rather than design expertise in the construction of this building.[3] Thus, Lathrop House and Allerton House exhibit varying degrees of involvement in design on the part of the associate architects.

A third case shows that sometimes an architect's name might be used, though little of his talent. Chicagoans McNally and Quinn were architects for 1500 Lake Shore Drive, with a spectacular penthouse designed as a Spanish Renaissance villa (cats. 35, 36). By the time they designed this, their masterpiece, they had been responsible for a number of high-rises in 1926 and 1927, at 70 East Cedar Street, 399 Fullerton Parkway, 1366 North Dearborn Street, and 3240 Sheridan Road. Rosario Candela, the New York associate architect for 1500 Lake Shore Drive had an equal number of tall buildings to his credit: the Stanhope Hotel at 997 Fifth Avenue (1927), 447 East 57th Street (1927), and 12 East 88th Street (1931) are a few that are extant. All of the drawings for 1500 Lake Shore survive and are in the holdings of The Art Institute of Chicago. Of the several hundred sheets of preliminary, presentation, and working drawings, not one was executed by Candela or his staff. His contract as associate also leads one to believe that his involvement in this 27-story luxury co-op, the largest done by McNally and Quinn at the time, was nominal but necessary to assure the investors of the high quality of the final product.[4]

These three instances recount varying relationships between New Yorkers and Chicagoans as principal and associate architects. A fourth case of interaction might be drawn from another Chicago high-rise apartment building of the 1920s—Ten West Elm Street by B. Leo Steif. First, however, a few general statements about the differences in apartment development between Chicago and New York might be helpful.

C. William Westfall has shown that typical Chicago apartment buildings (see figs. 11, 12; cat. 33) were low-rise, U-shaped courtyard structures that

Fig. 10 Murgatroyd and Ogden, Architects, with Fugard and Knapp, Associate Architects. Allerton House (now Allerton Hotel), 701 North Michigan Avenue, Chicago. 1924.

THE CAPITALS OF AMERICAN ARCHITECTURE

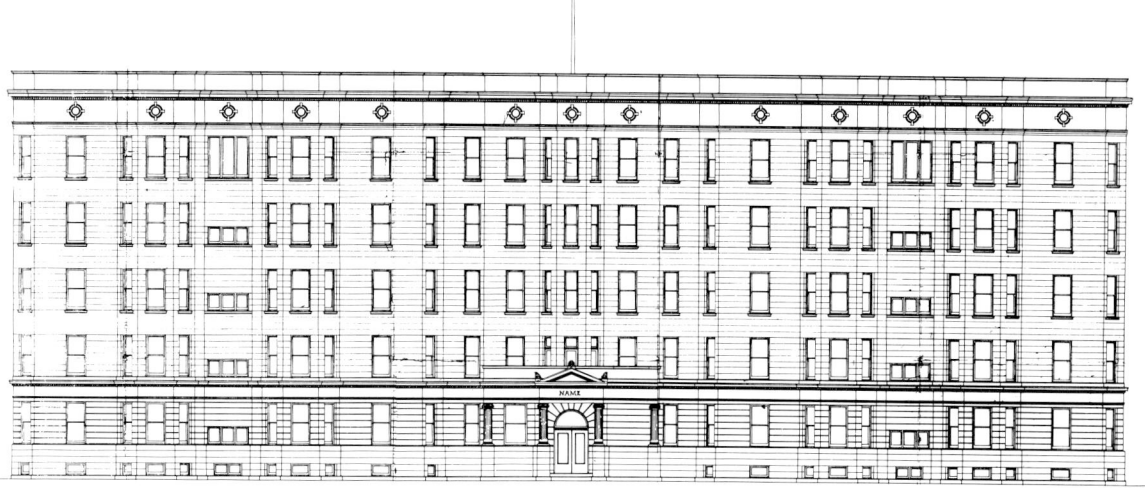

Fig. 11 Edmund R. Krause, Architect. Elevation of Lessing Apartments, 560-68 West Surf Street, Chicago. 1898-99. Department of Architecture, The Art Institute of Chicago.

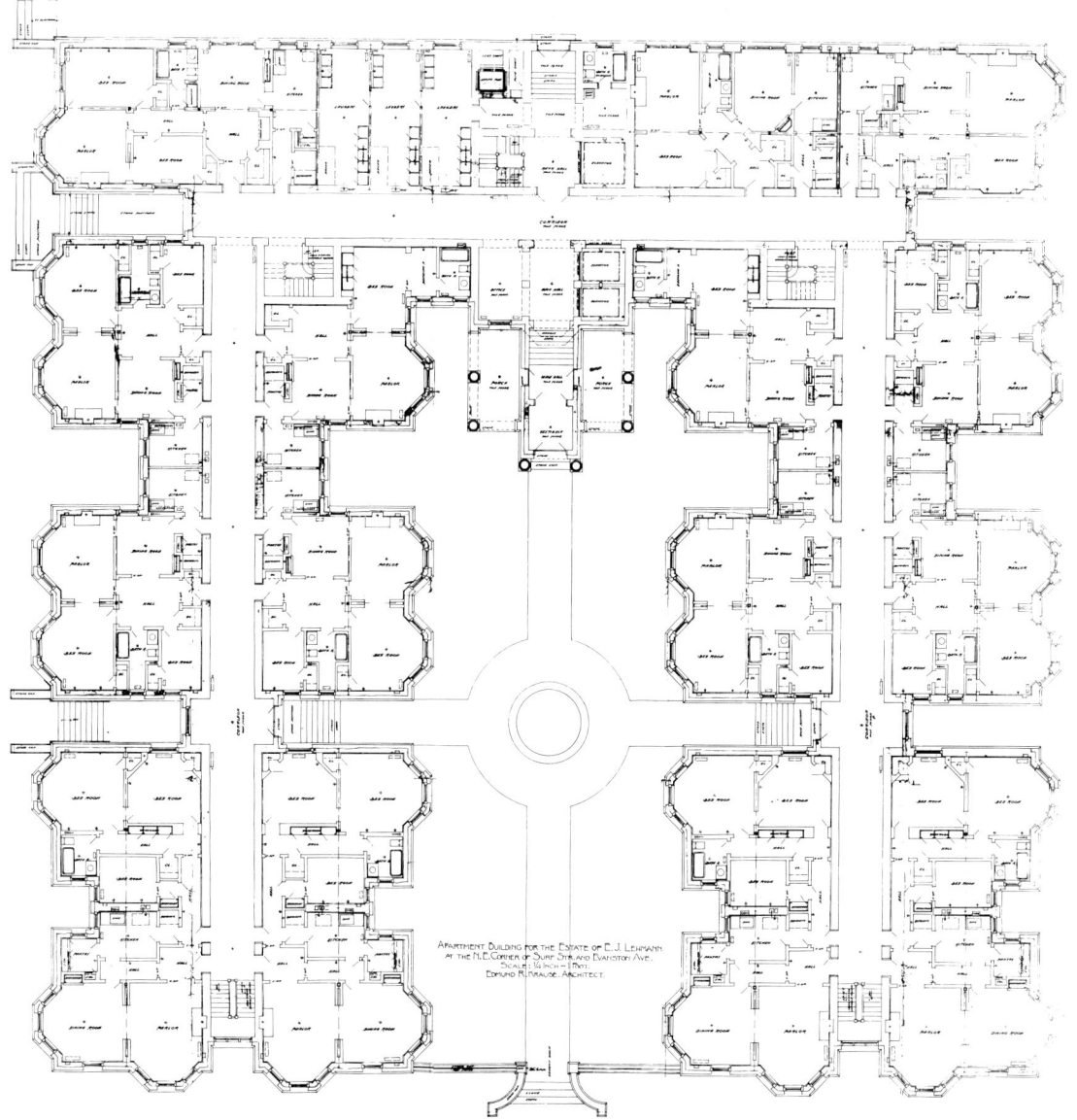

Fig. 12 Edmund R. Krause, Architect. Plan of Lessing Apartments, 560-68 West Surf Street, Chicago. 1898-99. Department of Architecture, The Art Institute of Chicago.

were considered roomier, homier, and more domestic, in the Anglo-American sense, than the more tightly spaced, stacked French flats popularized in New York after Richard Morris Hunt's Stuyvesant and Stephens Apartment houses from 1869 and 1871.[5] Chicago apartments from the late 19th and early 20th centuries were considered closer in style to Boston apartment houses. Chicago examples frequently used ground floor entrances of the so-called English and American basements of the 1880s, also popularized in the West Side row houses of New York architect and developer Clarence True.[6] But unlike the widespread intensification of density in Manhattan's large apartment blocks (see fig. 13; cats. 31, 32) smaller "deep court" apartments thrived in Chicago as housing for middle and working classes from the 1900s through the early 1920s.[7] During the same time period, luxury apartments based on New York's high-rises became increasingly popular in Chicago. The best example is 1550 North State Parkway (fig. 14) by Marshall and Fox, which originally had one apartment per floor, or ten apartments, each of about 8,000 square feet! Renaissance, Gothic, and Tudor high-rise apartments appeared sporadically in Chicago during the 1920s, for the wealthy as well as for the upper middle class.[8] Designed by architects like NcNally and Quinn, Rissman and Hirschfield, and Alfred Alschuler, these buildings in their increasing numbers compare with the profusion of Art Deco apartment towers for the middle class in New York, particularly in the Bronx's Grand Concourse and on the upper West Side near Central Park.

The twin-towered Century and San Remo apartments in New York (fig. 15, cat. 37) are linked, in Art Deco ornament though not overall design, to comparable middle-class apartment towers in Chicago — for example, B. Leo Steif's Ten West Elm (fig. 16). At the time of the completion of Ten West Elm in 1928, promotional material and newspaper articles likened it to the "modern French Style" of Art Deco, popular in New York. But the connection to New York is far more specific. In his notebook of studies for construction details for Ten West Elm, Steif had quickly sketched the elevations of two contemporary New York buildings: the Insurance Center at 80 John Street (Buchman and Kahn, 1926) and the Savoy Plaza Hotel (fig. 17). The chateau roof and polychrome brick and masonry of the Savoy Plaza are akin to a similarly massed roof and polychrome terracotta and brick in Steif's project. Although his sketch is undated, it is probable that these buildings, especially the Savoy Plaza, influenced the design of Steif's apartment tower.[9]

Fig. 13 *Right*. Henry J. Hardenbergh, Architect. Dakota Apartments, 1 West 72nd Street, New York. 1882-84. This photograph shows at the left Alfred Zucker's rarely seen Majestic Hotel (1889), 115 Central Park West, later the site of Chanin and Delamarre's Majestic Apartments (1929-30).

Fig. 14 Benjamin H. Marshall of Marshall and Fox, Architects. 1550 North State Parkway, Chicago. 1911.

THE CAPITALS OF AMERICAN ARCHITECTURE

Fig. 15 Irwin Chanin and Jacques Delamarre, Architects. The Century Apartments, 25 Central Park West, New York. 1929-31.

Fig. 16 Benjamin Leo Steif, Architect. Ten West Elm Street, Chicago. 1928.

Thus far we have seen four cases of specific interconnections between architects in Chicago and New York. All four deal with urban living, particularly high-rise apartment buildings, which were considered to be as distinctly American as commercial "skyscrapers."[10] It is the subject most likely to come to mind when one thinks of the architectural relationship between Chicago and New York. Within this development, the layered floors of blocky Chicago high-rises of the 1880s and 1890s—even when given an individual shape in New York as in Burnham's Flatiron Building (fig. 18)—contrast with the ornamented tower solution popularized in New York by Richard Morris Hunt's Tribune Building of 1876 and George B. Post's Equitable and Western Union buildings of the late 1870s and very early eighties (see fig. 19; cat. 45). At times, one can find the New York tower in Chicago, as in Richard Schmidt's Montgomery Ward Building of 1898 (cat. 54), whose Diana statue was inspired by the comparably terminated top of Stanford White's Madison Square Garden (fig. 20), and whose Venetian campanile may well relate to the later Metropolitan Life Tower in New York (1906-09) by Napoleon LeBrun and Son (fig. 21). The following essays by David Van Zanten and Carol Herselle Krinsky focus on those skyscraper developments in relationship to urban design and regional planning. Their discussions touch upon the architecture of institutions and transportation, which are featured in this exhibition, but detailed comparisons of the intercity interactions between industrial, health-care, theatrical, educational, and other building types await further investigation. Suffice it to say that, whether it is in commercial or residential buildings, the high-rise tower is the architectural image most often linked with Chicago, New York, and the American cityscape. As recent buildings in both cities demonstrate, the skyscraper, for residential and commercial purposes, is far from dead. Architects in both cities have begun to draw upon the high-rise imagery of the past in order to revitalize the steel and glass skyscraper.

In its Art-Deco, streamlined forms and setbacks Helmut Jahn's work reveals the influence of American architecture of the twenties. His Park Avenue

Fig. 17 McKim, Mead and White, Architects. Savoy Plaza Hotel, New York. 1926 (now demolished).

Fig. 18 D. H. Burnham and Co., Architects. Flatiron Building (formerly Fuller Building), 23rd Street, Broadway, and Fifth Avenue, New York. 1902.

THE CAPITALS OF AMERICAN ARCHITECTURE

Fig. 19 Photograph, c. 1880, of "Newspaper Row," New York, showing at right Richard Morris Hunt's New York Tribune Building, 1874.

Fig. 20 McKim, Mead and White, Architects. Tower, Madison Square Garden, New York. 1887-90 (now demolished).

Fig. 21 Napoleon LeBrun and Son, Architects. Metropolitan Life Tower, Madison Avenue and 23rd Street, New York. 1906-09.

THE CAPITALS OF AMERICAN ARCHITECTURE

Tower (cat. 5) will be on axis with the AT&T Building, whose great arcade, soaring shaft, and ornamented top (fig. 22) by Philip Johnson and John Burgee draw upon New York's heritage of masonry-clad skyscrapers from the late teens and early twenties. Like the AT&T Building, Robert A. M. Stern's "Late Entry to the Chicago Tribune Tower Competition" (cat. 64) is part of the theoretical tradition, popularized by Louis Sullivan, that considered the skyscraper as analogous to a column in that each has a distinct base, an uninterrupted shaft, and an ornamented top.[11] Stern's entry also derives its inspiration from Adolf Loos's famous column design in the Chicago Tribune Tower competition of 1922, a form that has also inspired Helmut Jahn's column design for 425 Lexington Avenue (cat. 65) next to the Chrysler Building in New York. Edward Larrabee Barnes's new Equitable Center also shows this newly revived interest in tripartite compositions with ornamented tops (cat. 66). Historical associations have also inspired recent apartment houses. In New York, the Gruzen Partnership has designed an apartment tower based on the San Remo by Emery Roth and Son (cats. 37, 38), which is currently under construction. Davis, Brody and Associates has likewise responded to the Art-Deco apartment house tradition of the upper West Side in a curved, streamlined design which, unfortunately, will not be built (fig. 23). In Chicago, Laurence Booth of Booth Hansen and Associates has designed and built an apartment tower at 320 North Michigan Avenue (fig. 24; cat. 39). Its poured concrete classical moldings, setback terraces, and wide "Chicago windows," all relate to earlier traditions. In a characteristically witty way, Stanley Tigerman's Pensacola Place II (fig. 25) incorporates in its east facade a Miesian exercise in glass, steel, and concrete, and on its west facade, a sequence of balconies that form a giant Ionic order, facing the graves of Chicago's great architects Sullivan, Burnham, and Mies van der Rohe in Graceland Cemetary.

In addition to the developing use of urban imagery in the projects of Chicago and New York architects, the competition between both cities for the tallest building in the world has gone on for more

Fig. 22 Philip Johnson with John Burgee, Architects. A T & T Building, 550 Madison Avenue, New York. 1981-83.

25

Fig. 23 Davis, Brody and Associates, Architects. Proposed Condominium Tower for 2000-2016 Broadway, New York. 1982. Rendering by Thierry Despont.

Fig. 24 Booth Hansen and Associates, Architects. 320 North Michigan Avenue, Chicago. 1981-83.

than a decade. The New York control of this record from 1918 through 1974 with the Woolworth, Chrysler, Empire State (fig. 26), and World Trade Center buildings was foiled by Chicago's Sears Tower (fig. 27). In 1982 New York developer Harry Helmsley expressed his desire to construct a building taller than the Sears's 1,454 feet, but Chicago architects Bruce J. Graham (of Skidmore, Owings and Merrill) and Harry Weese have recently designed structural systems that would more than double that height if given the opportunity to build. Continued competitive experimentation with the structure and imagery of the skyscraper in Chicago and New York indicates that this American creation will still be very much a part of our environment through the end of this century.

One final observation can be made about urban imagery in relation to Chicago and New York as we approach the close of this century. Both cities have hosted world's fairs that have made architectural history. New York's Crystal Palace and Latting Observatory of 1852-55 (cat. 67) incorporated the first passenger elevator, foreshadowing its later commercial use. More important, it brought to America the concept of the great iron and glass exposition hall of London's 1850-51 Crystal Palace, setting the stage for comparable glass exhibition spaces such as Chicago's lakefront center of 1876 and exhibition buildings at other world's fairs, including Chicago's World's Columbian Exposition of 1893. The plastered exteriors of the glass and steel sheds of Chicago's so-called "White City," discussed by both Van Zanten and Krinsky, were important for their uniform cornice lines, consistently classical detailing, and grouping around a Court of Honor (fig. 43), setting the tone for the City Beautiful movement as popularized throughout the nation by the city planning team of Chicagoans Daniel H. Burnham and Edward H. Bennett. The planners for the 1933 Century of Progress Exposition in Chicago chose an asymmetrical, decentralized plan for their fair (fig. 73), which, in contrast to Burnham's fair with the centralized Court of Honor, reflected America's hopes about the suburb and the expanded use of the automobile. Highlights of the '33 fair were various suburban "Homes of Tomorrow," which reappeared, in concept, in the Town of Tomorrow in New York's 1939 World's Fair (see figs. 74, 75; cat. 77). Many peo-

Fig. 25 Stanley Tigerman, Architect. West Facade, Pensacola Place II, 4334 North Hazel Street, Chicago. 1978-81.

ple are familiar with the famed Trylon and Perisphere (fig. 28) from the '39 fair because they served as the basis for a world of souvenir reproductions. Aside from the notoriety of fan dancer Sally Rand, there is no comparable architectural image, no single architectural association with Chicago's 1933 fair, perhaps because the centerpiece of that exposition was never built: Ralph Walker's Tower of Water and Light, a symbolic skyscraper (cat. 75). Even the much-criticized 1964 fair in New York had a distinct symbol in the stainless steel Unisphere, still standing in Flushing Meadow Park. Chicago is preparing for the 1992 World's Fair, to be called "The Age of Discovery," and Bruce J. Graham, of Skidmore, Owings and Merrill, the official architectural planner of the fair, is consulting with architects in Chicago, Los Angeles, and New York in an effort to coordinate fair design efforts, much as Burnham did a century ago. Perhaps these architects can use the discussions on architectural cooperation, competitive interaction, and urban imagery in this exhibition and in this volume when they design the urban symbol of the 1992 World's Fair, among their other projects. The work published here is, we hope, an introduction to future discussion of the architectural interaction between Chicago and New York. Current architectural talent in both cities indicates that this interchange, with its substantial impact on the American cityscape, will last into the next millenium.

Fig. 26 Shreve, Lamb and Harmon, Architects. Empire State Building, 350 Fifth Avenue, New York. 1931.

Fig. 27 Bruce J. Graham and Fazlur Khan of Skidmore, Owings and Merrill, Architects. Sears Tower, South Wacker Drive between Adams and Jackson Streets, Chicago. 1974.

Notes

1. Carl W. Condit, *The Chicago School of Architecture: A History of Commercial and Public Building in the Chicago Area, 1875-1925* (Chicago, 1964), *Chicago, 1910-29: Building, Planning, and Urban Technology* (Chicago, 1973), and *Chicago, 1930-70: Building, Planning, and Urban Technology* (Chicago, 1974). Sarah Bradford Landau, "The Tall Office Building Artistically Reconsidered: Arcaded Buildings of the New York School, c.1870-1890," in *In Search of Modern Architecture: A Tribute to Henry-Russell Hitchcock*, ed. Helen Searing (New York, 1982), pp. 136-64. Robert A. M. Stern, Gregory Gilmartin, and John Massengale, *New York 1900: Metropolitan Architecture and Urbanism, 1890-1915* (New York, 1983). Robert Bruegmann's publications in this area include "The Tribune Tower Competition: The 1920s Metropolis," *Inland Architect* 24 (June 1980), pp. 18-22, and "Holabird & Roche and Holabird & Root: The First Two Generations," *Chicago History* 9 (Fall 1980), pp. 130-65. See Gerald Larson, "Fire, Earth, and Wind: Technical Sources of the Chicago Skyscraper," *Inland Architect* 25 (Sept. 1981), pp. 20-37, for a sample of his forthcoming book. Paul Goldberger's *The Skyscraper* (New York, 1981) is the best published summary of its history, and Ada Louise Huxtable, in "The Tall Building Artistically Reconsidered," *The New Criterion* 1 (Nov. 1982), pp. 1-25, strongly criticizes contemporary efforts at imagery. See Andrew Alpern, *Apartments for the Affluent* (New York, 1975). Wim de Wit's work on Chicago apartments will be an exhibit at the Chicago Historical Society opening concurrently with this Chicago and New York show. Cf. C. William Westfall, "The Golden Age of Chicago Apartments," *Inland Architect* 24 (Nov. 1980), pp. 18-26.

2. Leland M. Roth, *McKim, Mead and White* (New York, 1983), pp. 138,150.

3. Palmer Odgen, "The Chicago Allerton House," *Architectural Forum* 42 (May 1925), pp. 313-16. That the Fugard and Knapp collection in the Chicago Historical Society has no drawings for this building reinforces the observation that the design was the responsibility of Murgatroyd and Ogden. For their work with George B. Post and Sons on the Governor Clinton, see *American Architect* 133 (May 20, 1928), p. 698.

4. Contract between Rosario Candela and McNally and Quinn, October 2, 1928: "Mr. Candela agrees to make three or four more visits to Chicago, to vise the work done by McNally and Quinn to date, to criticize the work and specifications as they progress, and to meet with McNally and Quinn in New York at various intervals when required. For the above services McNally and Quinn agree to pay Rosario Candela the sum of $6,500.00." The Quinn Papers, Burnham Library of Architecture, The Art Institute of Chicago.

5. Westfall (note 1), pp. 18-26, cites "Some Apartments in Chicago," *Architectural Record* 21 (Feb. 1907), pp. 119-30. See also *The American Architect* 96 (Dec. 22, 1909), pp. 261-71, and *Architectural Review* (Boston), n.s., 5 (Oct. 1917), pp. 225-27, for comparisons of New York and Chicago apartments.

6. Sarah Bradford Landau, "The Row Houses of New York's West Side," *Journal of the Society of Architectural Historians* 34 (1975), p. 28. See also Montgomery Schuyler, "The New New York House," *Architectural Record* 19 (Feb. 1906), pp. 84-103.

7. Randolph William Sexton, *American Apartment Houses of Today* (New York, 1926), pp. 139-40. See *Directory to Apartments of the Better Class* (Chicago: Partridge and Bradley, 1917), pp. 94-95, 118; *Apartment Homes* (Chicago: Baird and Warner, 1931[?]). Cf. Robert A. M. Stern and Thomas Catalano, *Raymond Hood* (New York, 1982), p. 101, for his "deep court" project for a New York tenement.

8. The *Portfolio of Fine Apartment Homes* (Chicago: Baird and Warner, 1928) surveys these. See especially pp. 10-33, 39-61, 64-71, 76, 80-83, and 90-91, in relation to few lowrise buildings and even fewer "deep courts."

9. Robert Sidney, comp., Scrapbook of the Career of B. Leo Steif, c. 1954. Burnham Library of Architecture, The Art Institute of Chicago. See also *Hotel Planning and Outfitting* (Chicago and New York, 1928), p. 181. For the Century Apartments and similar Majestic Apartments, see Diana Agrest, ed., *A Romance with the City: Irwin S. Chanin* (New York, 1982), pp. 76-84.

10. Arthur E. Willauer, "The Modern Home in New York," *The American Architect* 96 (Dec. 22, 1909), p. 263.

11. Louis Sullivan, "The Tall Office Building Artistically Considered," *Inland Architect* 27 (May 1896), pp. 32-34, reprinted in *Kindergarten Chats and Other Writings* (New York, 1947).

Fig. 28 Harrison and Fouilhoux, Architects. Trylon and Perisphere, World's Fair, New York. 1939 (now demolished).

The Nineteenth Century: The Projecting of Chicago as a Commercial City and the Rationalization of Design and Construction

David Van Zanten

In this century New York and Chicago have been the only two cities in the United States with the "critical mass" of designers and the sophisticated infrastructure in their large firms to function as international centers. Their hegemony has been challenged periodically—by the brilliance in design of Louis Kahn and Robert Venturi in Philadelphia, for example, or by the efficiency of the firms of Welton Becket and William Pereira in California—but in the end the weight of sheer mass has always maintained their dominance. The big projects in Philadelphia, Boston, San Francisco, Houston, and Los Angeles are usually by national firms headquartered in New York or Chicago. The architecture of these two centers is not necessarily of interest because it is "good," but because it is *there*: a fact and a force that must be recognized.

It is, thus, difficult to approach Chicago architecture at the turn of the century because of the way in which it has been mythologized. It is pictured idealistically as a common enterprise marked simultaneously by order and genius. Remarkable individual artists like Louis Sullivan, Frank Lloyd Wright, and Mies van der Rohe are seen as contributors to a broader architectural tradition known since 1941 as the Chicago School.[1]

Indeed, the city's architecture was a great and impressive whole, and each of these three great designers did depict themselves as simple toilers for the transparent expression of commonly held values. In 1896 Sullivan presented his skyscraper solution as the result of his "belief that it is of the very essence of every problem that it contains and suggests its own solution." He continued, "It is not my purpose to discuss the social conditions; I accept them as the fact, and say at once that the designs of the tall office building must be recognized and confronted at the outset as a problem to be solved." Wright in 1908 declared that his work "is dedicated to a cause conservative in the best sense of the word."[2] Mies repeatedly intoned, "Build, don't talk."

Thus, these artists would appear to have sought to submerge themselves in their community and to have found their poetry precisely where, in 1894, the French writer Paul Bourget suspected it lay:

> There is so little caprice and fancy in these monuments [Chicago office buildings] and these streets that they seem to be the work of some impersonal power, irresistible, unconscious, like a force of nature, in the service of which man has been but a docile instrument. It is this expression of the overpowering immensity of modern commerce which gives to the city something of tragedy and, to my feeling, of poetry.[3]

Harriet Monroe cited these words in 1896 when writing the biography of her brother-in-law, the architect John Wellborn Root. In 1941 Siegfried Giedion quoted them again: "The spirit of the Chicago School," he added in amplification, "its impulsion toward the simplest and most self-evident solutions, soon dominated the entire Loop. Its works sprang up one beside the other."[4]

It is thus under the powerful influence of these judgments that Chicago architecture has been studied—as a single phenomenon in which genius seemed to accommodate itself to order and order to genius, giving observers confidence that this ideal might be achieved in our own age.

I.
Since the city's founding (1833), Chicago building and land development has moved in exaggerated cycles of boom and bust. Homer Hoyt chronicled this movement carefully in 1933 and demonstrated the profile of a great boom coincident with the development of the skyscraper during the years between 1889 and 1893, a boom that abruptly terminated with the completion of the World's Columbian Exposition and the contemporaneous bank crash.[5] It was during this half-decade that most of the great early steel-framed, masonry-clad skyscrapers that are remembered today were built: Jenney's Manhattan Building (1889-90), second Leiter Building (1889-91), and Fair Store (1890-91); Holabird and Roche's Tacoma (1887-89) and Marquette (1893-95); Burnham and Root's Rand McNally (1889-90), Reliance (1890-95), and Marshall Field Annex (1891-93); as well as, of course, Adler and Sullivan's Schiller Building (1891-92) and Stock Exchange (1893-94, the last two reflecting the great solution of the Wainwright Building in St. Louis of 1890-91). During this busy half-decade, annual expenditure on building in Chicago jumped from $20,350,800 in 1888 to $25,065,500 in 1889, then to $47,322,100 in 1890, to $54,001,800 in 1891 and $63,463,400 in 1892, before dropping back to $28,517,700 in 1893 and finally to $19,100,050 in 1900.[6] The products of this boom entered literary consciousness in Henry Blake Fuller's *Cliff Dwellers* (1893) and surprised visitors to the Columbian Exposition, who discovered them uplake from that amazing confection. Sometimes, as in the cases of the New York critic Montgomery Schuyler and the Frenchman Paul Bourget, they preferred the skyscrapers to the fair.[7] The work of these five years in the Loop planted Chicago firmly in the public mind not only as a place where there was something totally new, but also as a place where that newness

was at war with itself. The art of the fair was pitted against the business of the skyscraper: the "rationality" of Sullivan against the "dream city" of Daniel H. Burnham's designer Charles B. Atwood. Suddenly, Chicago was a microcosm of the new world of architecture in all its aspects and factions.

There were, however, a number of stages in the history of Chicago architecture preparatory to this amazing half-decade of 1889-93. First, there was the settlement of Chicago itself, the effort to establish a city that at least until 1929 remained a matter more of optimistic projection than of static, proven reality. This repeated projection of Chicago emanated from that most basic and worrisome foundation stone of American optimism: boundless hope inspired by limitless increase in land value. Certain small parcels of the featureless American hinterland have always been perceived to be potentially productive of staggering speculative wealth. The first problem, however, was always how to locate these particular parcels—how to distinguish section 9, township 39, range 14 (put up for auction on September 4, 1830, and soon to be the Loop in Chicago) from a similarly featureless parcel of prairie in a similar geographical location, for example, near Lake Calumet. The second problem was, once one had chosen the parcel, to convince everyone else that yours was indeed distinct from others and so to begin to realize its projected value by subdivision, mortgage improvement, and stock issue.[8]

Thus the projection of something more than what actually existed was the basic idea that engendered Chicago and fueled its cycles of prosperity. The projection of what Chicago could be, however, evolved slowly, from one stage to another. In its first stage, the city was projected as a settlement of two-story brick and wooden blocks at the mouth of the contemplated Illinois and Michigan Canal that would connect the Great Lakes and the Mississippi basin. Hope of this waterway being realized gave impetus to Chicago's first boom, from 1833 to 1836, when handsome sums changed hands in consideration of empty lots. A parcel worth $100 in 1830 brought $50,000 in 1836. This was a paper boom, of course. The canal construction went slowly, the State of Illinois overextended itself, the depression of 1837 hit, and the bubble burst. In February 1842, the State Bank of Illinois failed. By then the total value of land in Chicago had fallen from its 1836 value of $10 million to $1.4 million.[9]

Recovery came late in the 1840s, first with the completion of the canal (1843-48), then with the construction of a railroad network centering on the city. The Galena and Chicago Union Railroad was commenced westward in 1848; the Illinois Central incorporated in 1851; the Rock Island started westward to Joliet in 1852 and crossed the Mississippi in 1855; the Michigan Central and the Michigan Southern entered the city in 1852. Another boom developed, but now a more solid one: a boom in buildings and services, hotels, hardware stores, and grain elevators. Lots changed hands with confidence that they would be built up to four stories in brick with cheap yellow Joliet limestone facing (oftentimes leftover from the canal excavation). The projected vision of the city achieved some substance now, and ornamental architecture arrived. In 1844 a number of businessmen promised the carpenter John M. Van Osdel their patronage if he would set himself up as an architect. He did so, drew an elevation for a four-story block on Lake Street, and charged $100 for his effort, "which," he later reminisced, "the owner considered a very large price for such an ordinary picture."[10] By the mid-1850s a dozen architects were busy in the city, some of them former carpenters and builders from the East like Van Osdel, Edward Burling, and William Boyington; others were German immigrants like Otto Matz and

Fig. 29 John M. Van Osdel, Architect. Cook County Courthouse and City Hall, Chicago. 1848-53; third story and remodeled cupola, 1858 (now demolished).

Frederick Baumann who claimed technical training in Europe.[11] These men could grasp the vision of a small provincial city, and they realized it in such buildings as Van Osdel's second County Courthouse, neither bigger nor smaller, better nor worse, than dozens like it erected during that decade in the Midwest (fig. 29; for comparison, see New York's City Hall, a veritable palace of government, fig. 30). Chicago at this point was the passive receiver of architecture, whether through the medium of a man like Van Osdel, trained in the East, or more dramatically in the form of whole facades of cast iron designed, fabricated, and shipped from New York by Daniel D. Badger and James Bogardus (see fig. 31), and looking like their Eastern counterparts (see cats. 41, 42).[12]

The projecting and envisioning of the future Chicago received another severe shock with the depression of 1857. Building activity fell from a total of $6,423,518 in that year to $3,246,400 the following year, and dropped to only $525,000 in 1862. That low figure also reflected another disrupting force, the Civil War. After an initial shock, however, the war caused Chicago to emerge as a more powerful economic entity, as Western economic activity

Fig. 30 Mangin and McComb, Architects. City Hall, New York. 1802-11.

Fig. 31 John M. Van Osdel, Architect. Page Brothers Building, Southeast corner of State and Lake Streets, Chicago. 1872. This print shows the building before later alterations.

shifted northward and as agriculture was displaced by manufacturing. A third great building and land boom took flight between 1863 and 1873, and the vision of Chicago as a great metropolis—the capital of the Midwest and potentially equal to New York or even to Napoleon III's Paris—was formulated and cautiously believed. Building activity increased to $2.5 million in 1863, $4.7 million in 1864, $14 million in 1869, and finally after the fire of October 7-9, 1871, to $40,133,600 in 1872 and $25,500,000 in 1873.[13]

The modest, industrious Van Osdel with his "ordinary picture" of 1844 had encapsulated the provincial urban vision of the second boom. Now in the third boom a new figure emerged, more cosmopolitan and self-assured: that of Major William Le Baron Jenney.[14] He cut a figure as no architect had before in Chicago. He understood the entrepreneurial vision of the city as well as any businessman-speculator and became thoroughly immersed in it. As business and speculation were what made Chicago remarkable, the deeper Jenney became involved in these, the more important and original became his work.

Jenney is usually remembered as he was depicted in Sullivan's *Autobiography* of 1924:

> The Major was a free-and-easy cultured gentleman, but not an architect except by courtesy of terms. His true profession was that of engineer.... Louis soon found out that the Major was not, really, in his heart, an engineer at all, but by nature, and in toto, a bon vivant, a gourmet. He lived at Riverside, a suburb, and Louis often smiled to see him carry home, by their naked feet, with all plumage, a brace or two of choice wild ducks, or other game birds, or a rare and odorous cheese from abroad.[15]

His partner W. B. Mundie had expressed similar observations more gently in 1914:

> Kindly, gracious, considerate, even to the least of his draftsmen.... It is said that he was never jealous of any man, and it is doubtful if any architect was jealous of him, which is unusual. Always jolly, an authority on good eating, a lover of a good story and a teller of hundreds of them, friend of great men and the waiter who served him, he was beloved by all he met. His democracy of action was as wide as his democracy of thought; he would address the architects of the world on involved scientific propositions, or slip into the kitchen of his club and gravely instruct the chef in the art of preparing a certain dish to be served.[16]

This picture of Jenney is as illuminating as it is amusing. The Major's social, educational, and economic pretenses were revolutionary among the humble confraternity of architects in Chicago around 1870. He was the son of a wealthy shipowner from Fairhaven (New Bedford), Massachusetts, and had had six different ancestors on the Mayflower.[17] He had been educated at Exeter and Harvard—in engineering at the Lawrence Scientific School—and between 1853 and 1856 had earned a diploma at the Ecole Centrale des Arts et Manufactures at Paris. He had excellent connections and upon graduation was invited into various speculative enterprises: as engineer of a projected railway across Mexico at the Isthmus of Tehuantepec (in 1856-57); as engineer of a mechanical bakery for the French army (1857-58); then as engineer for the Cincinnati and Marietta Railroad; and finally as prospective Paris agent for the Bureau of American Securities under the presidency of William Tecumseh Sherman. The Civil War broke out as Jenney was negotiating this last proposition, and—upon Sherman's advice—he had himself attached to Grant's staff as an engineer. In this capacity he rose to the rank of major and met a number of men important to his later career, especially General Arthur Charles Ducat.[18]

In 1868 Jenney settled in Chicago and established himself in the partnership of Jenney, Schermerhorn and Bogart. This was no mean grouping: Louis Y. Schermerhorn had been educated in engineering at the Rensselaer Polytechnic Institute and Union College and would go on to conduct major railroad and canal projects before ending his career as president of the American Dredging Company of Philadelphia. John Bogart, a graduate of Rutgers, would have a wide practice in railroad construction. Both had worked previously as landscape engineers in Brooklyn, Schermerhorn as division engineer for the construction of Prospect Park, Bogart as Chief Engineer of the Brooklyn Park Commission.[19] The firm immediately became involved in two of the most important real estate developments in Chicago. In 1869 three park commissions had been created free of city control, and Jenney, Schermerhorn and Bogart was employed to lay out an impressive series of parks and boulevards beyond the built-up area to the north, south, and west. Their designs had all the boldness of Baron Haussmann's plans for Paris but were laid out on vacant land so that the parks and boulevards, instead of having to be cut through an existing urban fabric, were to be enclosed by miles of new building visible chiefly in the speculators'

minds and on Jenney, Schermerhorn and Bogart's plans. The project was a success, however, especially in the west—lots were sold, houses were built, and profits made before the crash of 1873.[20] At the same time, Jenney's firm was employed, in collaboration with Olmsted, Vaux and Company of New York, to lay out the suburb of Riverside (fig. 32) at a particularly attractive point on the Des Plaines River intersected by the Chicago, Burlington and Quincy Railroad.[21]

The remarkable scale and quality of these two planning schemes have long been recognized. Jenney, Schermerhorn, and Bogart were not pioneers, as Van Osdel had been, but experienced, Eastern professionals importing ideas that had been worked out in New York in the first American picturesque suburb, Llewellyn Park, New Jersey (1851), and in Frederick Law Olmsted's early projects, most notably Prospect Park in Brooklyn (1866). Both Olmsted in New York and this firm of young imitators in Chicago were attempting to remake the American metropolis in the image of London or Paris, on paper. It is illuminating to see how their plans were used. In 1869 Jenney's acquaintance General Ducat commenced publication in Chicago of a monthly journal named *The Land Owner*, "devoted to the landed interests, building and improvement," and claiming to be the first such journal in the country. It contained information about Chicago real estate developments, notices on sales and building activities, letters on events in other major cities, and two large wood-cut tract plans in each issue. Not surprisingly, the plans in the second number were devoted to the West Side parks and those of the third to Riverside. The unstated function of the journal was one that would make Ducat an immensely important and wealthy man by the 1880s: first, to enable national and even international participation in Chicago real estate

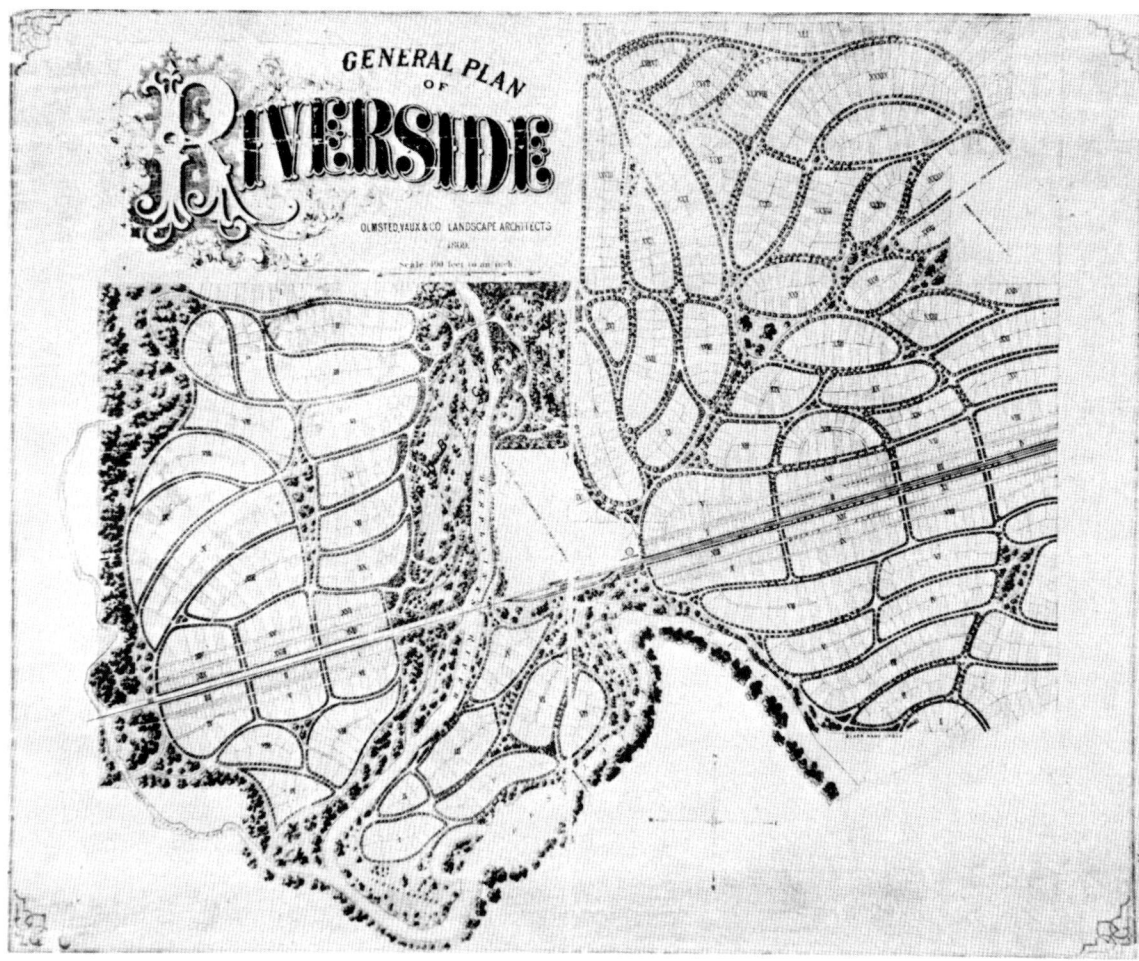

Fig. 32 Olmsted, Vaux and Co. General Plan of Riverside, Illinois. 1868.

speculation; second, to push specific projects in which Ducat or his friends and associates were interested. (Jenney, Schermerhorn, and Bogart all built in Riverside.) This was not a new form of real estate salesmanship; Daniel Boorstin has documented numerous cases of "cities" presenting themselves through newspapers even before they had been platted.[22] But this was a sophisticated version of the enterprise, requiring designs of national quality which only a firm like Jenney, Schermerhorn and Bogart could provide. What one wished to sell in Paris or New York had to look like Paris, or at least New York.

In 1869, just as the park project and Riverside were coming to fruition, Jenney left the partnership and entered an association with Sanford E. Loring as architect. Never behindhand, they immediately published a handsome book of designs with the pretentious title of *The Principles and Practice of Architecture*. Its 62 pages of text includes some simple but well-informed remarks about "first principles" and "truth in art." Again this was a professional style not seen before in Chicago. It was rewarded in 1872 with the commission for the Portland Block (fig. 33), a speculative office block built by an adventurous Boston investor, Peter Brooks. Brooks was later celebrated for the simplicity and efficiency that he demanded of his architects through his later Chicago agent, Owen Aldis, and the Portland Block set the tone. A contemporary newspaper reported, "The proprietor...is anxious to make this building remarkable for its solidity, perfect construction, convenient appointments, and elegant simplicity."[23] Its facades were of red, especially hard "pressed brick" with marble fittings, rather than of stone slabs, and the ornament was incised in the surfaces rather than run over the surface in pilasters and swags. W. B. Mundie remarked in 1914:

> The Portland Block was a radical departure from the then prevailing style in Chicago. Heretofore all the principal store and office buildings had been faced with stone. The Portland Block was pressed brick with elaborate stone trimmings. The idea of using brick in a fine office building was so new that the property owners in the vicinity, and the editor of the daily newspaper, protested, claiming that it would be an injury to the adjoining property. After completion, some of these, including the editor, stated that to their surprise the Portland Block was the handsomest building in the city.[24]

It was admiration for this building that caused Sullivan to seek employment with Jenney when he

Fig. 33 William Le Baron Jenney, Architect. Portland Block, Chicago. 1872 (now demolished). This print shows Jenney's original design, although only the first four stories were constructed as shown. Later additions were executed differently.

first arrived in Chicago in the winter of 1873, although he later discovered that it was Jenney's draftsman Adolph Cudell who had actually conceived the design.

The implication in the Portland Block that Jenney could satisfy a demanding client was borne out in the structure he erected for the notoriously contentious and stingy Levi Leiter in 1879 (fig. 34).[25] Not only was its brick and limestone exterior almost entirely devoid of ornament, but the windows were expanded to occupy so much of the wall area that Jenney devised a system to carry the weight of the floors on cast-iron columns, freestanding inside the exterior piers so that the latter had only to support their own weight. Its plain and efficient design was in stark contrast to the ornate, carved marble fretting of the building that Potter Palmer's architect E. S. Jennison had erected in 1868 and sold to Field, Leiter and Company. A change in taste had occurred around 1870, one partly influenced by the example of the Portland Block, but one also inspired by economic sensitivity. The Leiter Building had been erected after the third and most devasting crash in the city's history. Construction had fallen from $25,500,000 in 1873 to $5,785,541 in 1874, and did not rise above $10,000,000 until 1882. In 1877 the largest banks failed. Thousands were unemployed; battles were fought between workers, police, and troops in which twenty were killed. Chicago was a city now and the shock of economic collapse was greater. But there were also businessmen and journalists who pondered the misfortune and propounded lessons, especially in the pages of *The Real Estate and Building Journal* and *The Economist*. The speculation that had followed the Civil War was denounced as reckless, leaving injudiciously extravagant vestiges in the Field and Leiter store and Van Osdel's Palmer House Hotel. A new spirit of sobriety was counseled, one to be manifested in plain, solid brick construction.[26] The 1880s was a decade of economic caution, the first such in Chicago's history. Construction stood at $16,286,700 in 1882 and had only progressed to $20,350,800 (slightly below the level of 1873) in 1888. The style of the most prominent building—Beman's Pullman (cat. 46) or Burnham and Root's Rookery (fig. 35)—was simple and

THE NINETEENTH CENTURY

Fig. 34 William Le Baron Jenney, Architect. First Leiter Building, Chicago. 1879 (now demolished).

Fig. 35 Burnham and Root, Architects. Rookery Building, 209 South LaSalle Street, Chicago. 1885-86.

unornamented, in brick and sandstone. Today we would call it "Richardsonian," with decorative motifs in mind, but it was the "commercial style" to contemporaries who insisted that economy and practicality were the chief distinctions of Chicago buildings (although something very similar appeared contemporaneously, if not slightly earlier, in New York).[27] Between 1891 and 1896 the Goodspeed Publishing Company produced a six-volume study of the city entitled *Industrial Chicago*, the first two volumes of which were devoted to the "Building Interests." The anonymous authors hammered home that the "Commercial style is the title suggested by the great office and mercantile buildings now found here. The requirements of commerce and the business principle of real estate owners called this style into life. Light, space, air, and strength were demanded by such requirements and principles as the first objects and exterior ornamentation as the second."[28]

Such a "commercial style" was not a matter of motifs, as *Industrial Chicago* reiterated, but rather one of economic principle. It was in this area that Major Jenney made his most lasting contribution, the design and erection of the Home Insurance Building (fig. 36) in 1884-85, often considered the first skyscraper supported by a consistent metal skeleton.

Here we return to General Ducat. He had made his purpose not only the promotion of Chicago real estate, but also its protection. He had returned to military duty in 1877 to command the federal troops suppressing the riots of that year. Less dramatically, since 1856 he had reorganized and led Chicago's fire department. Such was his success that he received bids to serve as agent for a number of insurance companies in the East and abroad, seeking to "secure his influence and services exclusively at Chicago for that city and a large part of the West." In 1866 he accepted the offer of the Home Insurance Company of New York. In 1884 that company decided to erect a ten-story speculative office building on LaSalle Street, and Ducat asked Jenney for plans. The rest of the story Jenney told in a letter of April 19, 1897, written on the occasion of Ducat's death.

> The problem presented by the owners for the first time, was to erect on a very compressible soil a tall heavy building, divided above the second floor into a maximum number of small offices and necessitating a large number of windows of moderate size, reducing the piers between the windows to dimensions too small to carry the loads, if built of ordinary masonry; hence it became necessary to build metal columns in the piers. To avoid the inconvenience of expansion and contraction and to make the construction more homogeneous, the outside walls and floors were to be carried, story by story, independently on columns.

Ducat consulted frequently on the plans. When they were presented to the company building committee, Jenney was asked, "where was such a building?" "I responded this building would be the first.... As businessmen, they naturally asked how I knew that it would be successful and the best that could, under the circumstances, be devised?...I replied that I was ready to submit my designs and calculations to any eminent bridge engineers, that the construction resembled to a considerable extent iron railway bridges standing on end, side by side."[29] General Ducat, an engineer by training, stepped forward at this point and gave his assurance that Jenney's system was sound. The company building committee accepted, and the world's first metal skeleton "skyscraper"—the type of the Chicago building boom of 1889-93—came into being.

II.
Whether the Home Insurance Building was really the first skyscraper has often been questioned. The absence of the frame in the party walls has made some propose that Holabird and Roche's Tacoma Building (fig. 37) of 1887-89 was the first entirely skeletal skyscraper, but the presence of two massive brick walls inside that building has raised arguments for the priority of Jenney's own later Manhattan Building (1889) or Burnham and Root's Phoenix Building (1885-87) and Rand McNally Building (1889). Jenney's initial experiment in the Home Insurance Building was little-enough remarked that already in 1896 the journal *Engineering Record* inquired of its readers who had invented "the lofty steel construction of buildings." Daniel Burnham and the Chicago engineer Charles Louis Strobel re-

Fig. 36 William Le Baron Jenney, Architect. Home Insurance Building, Chicago. 1884-85 (now demolished). The top two stories and cornice were added in 1890.

THE NINETEENTH CENTURY

Fig. 37 Holabird and Roche, Architects. Tacoma Building, Chicago. 1887-89 (now demolished).

Fig. 38 George B. Post, Architect. Produce Exchange, New York. 1881-85 (now demolished).

sponded that it was Jenney in the Home Insurance Building, but other correspondents proposed the New York architect George B. Post, who had supported the light court walls of the Produce Exchange (fig. 38; cats. 47,48) on a metal frame already in 1881.[30] The matter is further complicated by the fact that in 1888 the Minneapolis architect Leroy Buffington patented the idea of a steel-framed skyscraper and initiated proceedings against a building owner, but lost the case when a pamphlet of 1884 by Frederick Baumann was produced that outlined the system already in that year. Baumann explained in a note on a copy of his pamphlet that is in the Ryerson and Burnham Libraries of The Art Institute of Chicago that he had intended to erect a building on the skeletal system on the southwest corner of Clark and Jackson Streets in 1883, but that his client had sold the lot instead.[31] He advanced the system again when making an unaccepted proposal for the Home Insurance project.[32]

The beauty of the steel frame was its own logic and, being logical, it was conceived—albeit imperfectly—by several men simultaneously. Sullivan wrote in his *Autobiography*:

In Chicago the tall office building would seem to have arisen spontaneously, in response to favoring physical conditions, and the economic pressure as then sanctified, combined with the daring of promoters.

[T]he Chicago activity in erecting high buildings finally attracted the attention of the local sales managers of Eastern rolling mills; and their engineers were set to work. The mills for some time past had been rolling those structural shapes that had long been in use in bridge work. Their own ground was thus prepared. It was a matter of vision in salesmanship based upon engineering imagination and technique. Thus the idea of a steel frame which should carry *all* the load was tentatively presented to Chicago architects. The architects of Chicago welcomed the frame and did something with it.[33]

The invention of the steel frame was inevitable, but the inventor would be a man both confident in his engineering and in his business relations with his clients. The right combination of factors first appeared in 1884 in the case of Jenney, Ducat, and the Home Insurance Company. Thus the frame system was tested, although tentatively, and not merely conceived, as in Baumann's case. But Jenney's strength was also his weakness: he was an old soldier, a *bon-vivant*, a member of the Union League Club like Ducat. As such, they were men of the 1860s and 1870s. A new generation that would displace them was emerging during the 1880s: Owen Aldis and William E. Hale would show keener instincts in real estate; the Commercial Club would rise above the stodgy Union League; Burnham and Root, Holabird and Roche, and Adler and Sullivan would prove themselves the most nimble artists of the steel frame. But it is important to note that most of these young architects had been trained in Jenney's office: Burnham, Holabird, Roche, Sullivan. To their number must be added the two most radical designers of the period, the Neo-Grec Adolph Cudell and the anarchist John Edelmann.[34] The only other office then in Chicago that contributed to training of architects of the great skyscraper boom was Carter, Drake and Wight, which was dominated by New Yorker Peter B. Wight and which employed both Burnham and Root upon Wight's arrival in 1871 (see cats. 43, 44). (Not inappropriately, if Jenney was an engineer who became an architect in Chicago, Wight was an architect who became an engineer of fireproof construction.)[35] It was Jenney and Wight, to the exclusion of Van Osdel and Boyington and Matz and Baumann, who had the urbanity, vision, and pretense to fire the ambitions of these brilliant young men.

The Tacoma Building, the first office building erected by Holabird and Roche (who had founded their firm in 1881) was still tentative in its structure, mixing cast iron with wrought iron and steel as well as using interior masonry walls for stability. But in its plan, elevations, and use of bay windows, it was infinitely simpler and more efficient than the Home Insurance Building, as was the manner of its construction carried out by the infant firm of general contractors, George A. Fuller. Two years later Burnham and Root (founded in 1873) began the Rand McNally Building—a square doughnut around a glazed light court—with a consistent steel frame supporting the party walls as well as the facades. The facades were no longer of heavy brick and stone masonry but of terracotta produced specifically to fit the frame. Jenney meanwhile showed his mettle in his Manhattan Building (1889-91), with a full steel frame and bay windows, and in his mammoth department stores, the second Leiter (1889-91) and the Fair Store (1890-91), each with extraordinarily broad bays and high ceilings.

These last, however, were still covered in heavy, expensive cut-stone masonry. Architectural terracotta was a lighter, cheaper, more solid material ornamented by repetitive molding rather than by hand carving. It also was produced locally by several large Chicago firms, the first of which had been the Chicago Terra Cotta Company, founded in 1868 under the direction of Jenney's sometime partner, Sanford Loring. (The 1898 *History of Real Estate, Building and Architecture in New York City* credits Chicago with first adopting the material, and it dates its appearance in New York very precisely to 1877.)[36] The combination of steel and terracotta introduced in the Rand McNally Building was perfected after Root's death by Burnham and his designer Charles Atwood in the transparent Reliance Building (1895) for the investor William Hale, and repeated in the Fisher Building of that same year. Holabird and Root's simple steel buildings—the Caxton, Pontiac, Monadnock extension, Marquette, and Old Colony —came to look overbuilt in comparison, and in 1898 they adopted a minimal terracotta cladding in the Cable Building, followed in 1899 by the McClurg Building.[37]

Nonetheless, to informed critics coming to Chicago at the beginning of the 1890s, it was neither Jenney, nor Burnham, nor Holabird and Roche that offered the most completely and cogently reasoned steel-framed buildings, but instead a firm founded in 1881, Adler and Sullivan. In 1890-91 they had erected the Wainwright Building (fig. 39) in St. Louis with a consistent steel frame and in 1891-92 the Schiller Building (cat. 50) in Chicago with ten stories of offices supported over a theatre in its base. The support the firm received from Montgomery Schuyler in the pages of the *Architectural Record* is well known.[38] Even more unequivocal and methodical was the contemporaneous campaign waged in their favor by the critic Barr Ferree in the pages of the popular *Engineering Magazine* from 1891 to 1897. This journal, which had been founded in New York to keep the general public abreast of science and engineering in all areas, immediately took up the matter of the skyscraper. The initial article on that topic appeared in the first volume (1891) by the New York architect John Beverly Robinson, who presented the steel frame as a wonder of modern technology and one known only in New York, in George Post's work, and especially in Bradford Lee Gilbert's Tower Building (fig. 40).[39] Soon after, however, Ferree came forward with monthly editorials on proper skyscraper design and with a series of pieces by Sullivan and his associates. First, in 1892, "Pessimism of Modern Architecture," by John Edelmann, illustrated with Sullivan's drawings of the Wainwright and Schiller buildings; then, also in 1892, Sullivan's "Ornament in Architecture" and Adler's "The Tall Office Building Past and Present" and "Light in Tall Office Buildings." Later Adler published two further articles on theatre design and, in January 1897, a final piece entitled "The Stimulus of Competition in Architectural Construction."[40]

Fig. 39 Adler and Sullivan, Architects, with Charles Ramsey, Associate Architect. Wainwright Building, 709 Chestnut Street, St. Louis. 1890-91.

Fig. 40 Bradford Lee Gilbert, Architect. Tower Building, 50 Broadway, New York. 1888-89 (now demolished).

Meanwhile Ferree was repeatedly reproducing and praising the firm's work—and Chicago architecture in general—in his editorials. In September 1892, he cited the city as the place where there "are more and better business buildings than are to be found in any equal area on the face of this earth." A few months later he announced the opening of the Schiller Building as "an event of more than local importance" and henceforth cited it as "the finest high building in the world" and the model upon which modern skyscraper design should evolve.[41] Finally in 1898, in a lengthy essay of his own published in the *Journal of the Franklin Institute,* Ferree methodically demonstrated the logical superiority of Adler and Sullivan's work on many grounds.[42] What Ferree found so praiseworthy, of course, was the frank practicality of Adler and Sullivan's work articulated rather than encumbered by art. He felt this a commercial architecture for a commercial age: "American architecture, as no other architecture is or was, is dominated today by commercialism.... Commercialism in itself is only the current form of the word 'practical'."[43] This is why, perhaps, Ferree published five articles by Adler and only one by Sullivan, for Adler demonstrated great practical subtlety in all the matters concerning the actual construction and renting of a commercial building: structure, foundations, planning, admission of light, integration of functions, urban amenity. One begins to realize in Ferree's presentation of Adler and Sullivan that the firm had not only evolved a particularly elegant expression of the steel frame in architectural decoration, but indeed a whole system of rational commercial building and urbanism. The Schiller building was its prototype, as Ferree so often reiterated, because here a major public space, the Schiller Theatre, was inserted in the base of a tall rental structure. Furthermore, the careful design of the deep mass provided light for the offices on both sides and opened the street at the tenth floor as it transformed itself into a narrow tower. The firm made an even more dramatic demonstration of their system in their project for the Fraternity Temple (fig. 41)—32 stories tall with two tiers of setbacks—published in September 1891. Sullivan extended it to a vision of an entire skyscraper city of towers rising above setbacks in an article published in that same year.[44] All of this demonstrated a broader grasp of the problem of commercial architecture than Jenney, Burnham and Root, or Holabird and Roche had shown, and reflected the thinking of Adler as much as Sullivan (as had the Auditorium of 1886-90, which was the embryo from which these ideas had sprung). Neither the Auditorium nor the Schiller Building would have been possible without Adler's structural ingenuity and acoustical brilliance as well as his practical sense of planning—reasons why he was hired by William B. Tuthill to consult on the design of New York's Carnegie Hall (fig. 42).

III.

There were two other important personalities that emerged during the Chicago building boom of 1889-93: Owen Aldis and George A. Fuller. The first was a building agent and manager, the second a general contractor. Both were contemporaries of Jenney's pupils (Aldis was born in 1853 and Fuller in 1852) and collaborated closely with them. Rationalization was the strength of these architects, and Aldis and Fuller were organizers and specialists of important new sorts. What is significant, however, is that they did not pretend to be architects and, while working with designers and other specialists, they began to intrude on the architects' professional turf, to hem them in. In Jenney's heyday, planning and construction had been as much the architect's job as design and he could adjust the three in relation to each other. But the emergence of the specialist also represented a quantum jump forward in the efficiency of architectural production and could be used by a powerful personality like Daniel Burnham to re-create and broaden the architect's function.

We have noted Jenney's skill in making Chicago real estate development an international enterprise and have mentioned how in 1872 he had built the stern but well-appointed Portland Block for the Boston investor Peter Brooks. In 1879 Brooks appointed Owen Franklin Aldis to manage the structure.[45] Aldis was a young lawyer (admitted to the Chicago bar in 1876) with excellent New England credentials, being the son and grandson of judges of the Vermont Supreme Court and a graduate of Yale (1874). He clearly inspired a great deal of confidence in the Brooks family, for he was soon set to work overseeing large investments in Chicago real estate and buildings. In 1880 Brooks's brother, Shepherd, had Aldis buy the lot south of the Portland Block and lease it to a builder to erect the Grannis Block, which he then purchased in 1884 (just before it burned in February 1885). In 1881 Aldis ventured directly into building when he served as the Brookses' agent for the erection of the Montauk Block, which was remarkable for its ten-story height, efficiency of design, fireproof red-brick construction, and lack of decoration. Aldis then served as agent for the family for the construction of the Rookery Building in 1885-86, acting as president of the Central Safe Deposit Company which they had created as builder and owner, and finally for the Monadnock Building, under discussion since 1881 and built from 1889 to 1891.

All of these buildings from the first phase of Aldis's career were designed by Burnham and Root, with whom Aldis had a warm relationship. The architects responded to the Brookses' often-reiterated demands for simplicity and efficiency. But just as the building boom accelerated, a change took place. Aldis went out on his own in 1888, founding Aldis, Aldis and Northcote (later Aldis and Company) with his brother, Arthur, a graduate of Harvard formerly engaged in ranching in Wyoming.[46] He carried on the Brookses investments, erecting the Monadnock extension in 1892-93, but also represented a broader series of corporate trusts. He employed a new, more efficient team of constructors, namely the architects Holabird and Roche and the general contractor George A. Fuller, building now only in steel. Coincidentally with the Monadnock extension, carried out in steel by Holabird and Roche rather than in masonry as Burnham and Root had done in the earlier section of the building, Aldis employed his team to erect the Pontiac Building (1889-91) for the Brookses, the Venetian Building (1893-94) for the Chicago Leasehold Trustees, and finally the Marquette (1893-94) for the Marquette Safety Deposit Company whose president was Aldis himself. Such was Aldis's success that by 1902 it was said that one-fifth of all Chicago office space was Aldis-produced or Aldis-managed; and the firm has carried on until today.[47]

Aldis thus emerged as a professional, specialized "client," first for Burnham and Root, then for Holabird and Roche, a methodical and demanding corporate transformation of Jenney's friend General Ducat. Aldis knew very well what he wanted and how the architect might provide it, as his office correspondence once made clear. He was not a client the architect had to break in each time; on the contrary, he was a predictable term in the equation whose only fault, perhaps, was that he usually wanted the same thing every time. This quality of consistency also characterized the third unit in the team, the George A. Fuller Company.[48] The founder of that name had been the office manager of the prestigious Boston architectural firm of Peabody and Stearns. In 1883 he had moved to Chicago to work as general contractor on the Grand Opera House.[49] His company proved itself in its particularly efficient erection of the Rookery Building for Aldis (1885-86) and of the Tacoma Building (1887-89). The company flourished in the building boom, erecting the Rand McNally Building, Women's Temple, Reliance Building, and Marshall Field Annex for Burnham, as well as the Schlesinger and Meyer Store for Sullivan

THE NINETEENTH CENTURY

Fig. 41 Adler and Sullivan, Architects. Fraternity Temple, Chicago. 1891 (unexecuted).

Fig. 42 William B. Tuthill, Architect, with Henry J. Hardenbergh, Associate Architect (for tower), and Dankmar Adler and William Morris Hunt, Consultants. Carnegie Hall, 57th Street and Seventh Avenue, New York. 1890-91.

41

and the series for Aldis already mentioned. Dwight Perkins and James Gamble Rogers, just commencing their careers, gratefully accepted Fuller's services for the erection of their small, early skyscrapers, Steinway Hall and the Lees Building. But the Chicago building boom was only Fuller's launching pad. The firm soon invaded the East, and between 1901 and 1903 erected the Flatiron Building (fig. 18; cat. 4; formerly the Fuller Building) on Broadway to Burnham's plans and moved their offices to the top floor. Paul Starrett declared that by 1910 80 percent of office construction in Manhattan was by Fuller.[50]

What did Fuller do to receive such a staggering proportion of the business? The firm took charge of all subcontracting, and delivered the building on a fixed date at a fixed price. It assumed contractual responsibility to vastly simplify the client's and architect's business. Most importantly, it did things well: its buildings were well built, on time, and within budget. Paul Starrett, one of the principals of the company and eventually its president, produced in his autobiographical reminiscences, *Changing the Skyline*, one of the most unrelenting chronicles of "can do" in that broad tradition of American literature. If we are to believe him, for example, Fuller contracted to build the Commodore Hotel in twelve months, got possession of the site three months late due to tardy rock excavation, but still opened the completed structure ninety days early. His chapter headings include "Blood and Steel," "Getting the Job," "Speed," and "Men."

By the end of the building boom of 1889-93, the Chicago architect found himself squeezed between the professional, specialized client in the person of Aldis and his fellows, and the corporate builder, Fuller and other general contractors. What was left for the architect was a very thin slice of responsibility, a slice that came all too near what Fuller depicted in the *Cliff Dwellers*: the design of ornamental doors and cornices for cubes of office space that were otherwise planned and erected by other specialists. We glimpse both the attraction and the defects of the system in Sullivan's single surviving professional letterbook covering the period April 2, 1902, to January 5, 1905, the period of the completion of the Schlesinger and Meyer Store by George A. Fuller.[51] This correspondence is almost exclusively with the Fuller Company. Sullivan requested bids on the kitchen equipment. He sent specifications and asked Fuller to solicit prices. Sullivan wanted doors redesigned and "suggest[ed]" Fuller get the contractor to lower his bid. And so on. It was like shadowboxing: rarely did Sullivan come into direct contact with the subcontractors actually executing his designs. He approved of everything, was informed of everything, but it was always filtered through the Fuller Company. The fear that clients expressed when Sullivan broke with Adler in 1895 that his office could no longer provide the necessary engineering services could have been allayed by the presence of Fuller, but at this price.[52] We have noted how in his *Autobiography* of 1924 Sullivan attributed the invention of the skyscraper to steel fabricators and real estate speculators. In 1916, he had attributed responsibility for the modern office building specifically to Aldis and to another real estate man, William Hale.[53] This sense of helplessness is echoed in his 1902-05 letterbook. In the *Cliff Dwellers*, the architect of the skyscraper, Atwater, keeps his office at the top of the building, but turns from commercial architecture to house design out of genteel frustration on the restrictions to his creativity.

The situation became such that one wonders why there were architects at all in Chicago after 1900. Would it have not been more efficient for either Aldis or Fuller to institute a specialized design department (as, indeed, some builders had done already, like Wilson Brothers or the Ballinger Company in Philadelphia)? The answer on one level is simple: the architect had become a legal necessity. According to the Chicago Building Code, every building over two stories in height or more than 1,250 square feet in area had to be presented by an architect to the City Building Commissioner before any contracts could be let.[54] The architect, in turn, had to be licensed in the State of Illinois, according to a law of June 3, 1897. (This was the first licensing law for architects in the nation; it was not until April 28, 1915, that New York required architects to be registered. A later law granted licenses to all architects in practice before April 12, 1929.) That licensing law served the architects by establishing a professional monopoly for them just when they were being most closely pressed by developments in the building industry, but it also served a corporate end by concentrating legal liability on them. Henceforth any mistake or knavery on the part of the contractors or any miscalculation in the technical conceptualization of the building was the architect's responsibility unless he could prove otherwise.

Fig. 43 Court of Honor at the World's Columbian Exposition, Chicago. 1893 (now demolished).

The architects would not seem to have found mere legal existence satisfying. They had to find some way to assert and expand their authority between these impinging forces in order to gain imaginative space for themselves, and a solution existed in the economic situation itself. In 1889 Congress authorized Chicago (in preference to New York and other competitors) to set itself firmly before the world as a great industrial center and a good investment by organizing the Columbian Exposition that would open in May 1893. Burnham had himself appointed Chief of Construction, Root Consulting Architect, and F. L. Olmsted and Company Consulting Landscape Designers. Ducat's trumpeting of Jenney's plans by fold-out pages in *The Land Owner* were nothing compared to this. Root was initially to be the sole architect, conceiving a huge arcaded courtyard open at its far end to the lake—abubble with a great fountain in a central basin and defined by exotic Romanesquoid structures in steel and colored terracotta that we glimpse tantalizingly in his few surviving sketches (see cats. 70, 71). The building committee, however, insisted on a board of architects, and Burnham selected five well-known Eastern firms: Richard Morris Hunt; McKim, Mead and White; George B. Post; Peabody and Stearns; and Van Brunt and Howe. Later, five Chicago architects were added to the list. Now, achieving unity emerged as the primary problem, and the architects agreed to work within a strict framework: a common envelope derived from Root's model, a common cornice line, a common style (i.e., the "classical"), and continuous colonnades toward the court. At the conclusion of their first meeting in Chicago in January 1891, Root caught pneumonia and died, but his vision had already been transformed into the "White City" that was to thrill the public and the profession upon its completion in 1893 (fig. 43; cat. 70). Burnham carried on as Chief of Construction—the architects having agreed at the outset to surrender all authority over execution of their designs—and employed the retiring Charles Atwood from New York for incidental designs, proving to himself that art could be successfully compartmentalized and delegated like engineering or construction.[55]

The picture of Burnham as the "Captain of Architecture" has come down to us in many forms: his posed portraits, his palatial estate beside Lake Michigan in Evanston, and his aphorism "Make no little plans, they have no magic to stir men's blood and probably themselves will not be realized." Harriet Monroe depicted Burnham after Root's death pacing his deceased colleague's living room and raging, "I have worked, I have schemed to make us the greatest architects in the world. I have made him see it and kept him at it—and now he dies—damn! damn! damn!"[56] On a quieter note, Paul Starrett dated the commencement of his career as the greatest builder of the 20th century from Burnham's remark to him in the drafting room, "This note taking about concrete and steel window frames is all very well, but don't you know that you can hire any number of civil engineers, mechanical engineers, and electrical engineers, who will be absolutely contented to spend their whole lives in doing routine?...You have a genius for organization and leadership. My advice to you is to drop all this note taking. Study the organizational side of the business."[57] Sullivan summed it up in his *Autobiography*:

> During this period there was well underway the formation of mergers, combinations and trusts in the industrial world. The only architect in Chicago to catch the significance of this movement was Daniel Burnham, for in its tendency toward bigness, organization, delegation, and intense commercialism, he sensed the reciprocal workings of his own mind.

Again, Sullivan remembered Burnham intoning "Think of a man like Morgan who could take a man like Cassatt in the palm of his hand and set him on the throne of the Pennsylvania."[58]

Burnham made room for himself between the managers and the general contractors by becoming a "Captain of Architecture," a man who could guide designers of the reputation of Hunt, Post, and McKim in the fulfillment of a single, great project. And the Court of Honor of the Columbian Exposition finally created (if only momentarily) the great set of public buildings Chicago had previously so signally lacked. Here, finally, was a place symbolizing Chicago where one could wander and glory in the idea of the city, as previously one could do only at Versailles or Nymphenburg.

The complication, of course, is that Burnham accomplished this through the employment of East Coast (especially New York) architects working in what was considered to be an East Coast style of classicism. Sullivan refused to cooperate. When he was tardily invited to participate, he designed his Transportation Building in wonderful red, green, and gold "Sullivan ornament," recalling Root's initial projects for the fair and striking a jarringly discordant note behind the cool white colonnades of the Court of Honor. But what had Burnham really imported from New York? He had been careful in his initial letters to the architects to state that they would provide designs only and would have no authority over the execution of their work. He was clearly not so overawed by Hunt's, Post's, and McKim's professional efficiency that he would seek their active participation in matters of erection. This is striking because these very architects were the founders of the first large offices in America: they had been producing large projects in great volume already in the 1880s. By 1900 McKim, Mead and White in particular could produce designs of a variety and quality quite above that of the repetitive, often gauche productions of Burnham's office. But the East Coast offices were more loosely organized —"like an atelier," as Leland M. Roth has observed of McKim, Mead and White.[59] What Burnham valued was office efficiency. The East Coast offices were Burnham's inspiration, but not his precise model. Instead, his vision of an organized operation would seem to have owed more to the elemental corporate models provided by Morgan and Rockefeller—New Yorkers still, but New Yorkers uninfected by the aristocratic cult of artistic form. What Burnham clearly wanted from the Easterners in 1890 were sheets of delicate ornamental facades suffused with the taste and tradition of the oldest part of the nation. No architect in Chicago had the background to produce such essays in architectural good breeding and unobjectionableness. But Burnham remained suspicious that the Eastern attachment to tradition might lead to over-refinement if it were not managed with Chicago breadth and rationalization. His conduct suggests a saying of the period, "When Chicago gets ahold of culture, culture will have to hum."

IV.

We have not yet noted one of the great peculiarities of the Chicago School: its almost complete restriction to office buildings or department stores with hotels and apartment buildings as a secondary focus. These architects were the best-born, best-trained, and best-connected in the city, and yet they were satisfied with this single field of endeavor. Their contemporaries in Europe were mostly government architects erecting museums, like Charles-Louis Girault in Brussels and Paris, or government offices, like Otto Wagner in Vienna. The fair buildings would seem to have demonstrated what the academic critics never tired of reiterating: that public buildings were the only truly artistic works of architecture because they alone could communicate profound ideas about the community. The fair thus poses the question of why public architecture had not come forward before as the escape from the architect's dilemma in commercial design.

There were, of course, major public buildings in Chicago in 1893: the City and County Building (1875-85) by J. J. Egan, for example, and the Federal Building by the Supervising Architect of the Treasury of 1879. The construction of both had been accompanied by scandal and litigation. They were vastly expensive, badly planned and built, and both were replaced within a few decades of their erection.[60] There were also architects in Chicago specializing in public work, specifically John C. Cochrane who designed the state capitol in Springfield, as well as numerous county courthouses between the time of his arrival in Chicago in 1855 and his death in 1887.[61] In addition, the Chicagoans M. E. Bell and W. J. Edbrooke served as Supervising Architect of the United States Treasury from 1883 to 1887 and 1891 to 1893, respectively. Bell claimed to have produced 42 major designs during his tenure.[62] But these were clearly not the most distinguished practitioners in Chicago at the time, and the reason why is made very plain in the utter corruption revealed, for example, in the construction of the City and County Building. Later, between 1905 and 1910, Dwight Perkins served as architect of the Chicago School Board and finally resigned amid lawsuits and recriminations. The shenanigans of government officials and government contractors is one of the minor themes of Paul Starrett's reminiscences, *Changing the Skyline*.

Thus one of the remarkable achievements of Burnham's fair was the demonstration that building on a public scale could be carried out by good architects. Among Burnham's techniques to accomplish this was the elimination of the government from the project: the fair was carried out by a chartered stock corporation directed by businessmen rather than politicians. It thus demonstrated that corporate structure permitted private enterprise to balance and even dominate the corrupt public system and thus made room for the best-trained architects to realize something of their ambition.

We have used the word "corporate" three times in specific cases in this essay. We have mentioned how Owen Aldis used the stock company to invest East Coast money in Chicago real estate. We have seen how George A. Fuller simplified the erection of buildings by creating a structure of planners and expediters taking complete financial responsibility. Finally, we have seen how a great public project, the Columbian Exposition, could be carried out free from political intrigue. The corporation was a new thing in late 19th-century America. Earlier in the century corporations had been restricted to public works—for example, canals and railroads. Its principles—the pooling of resources, the limitation of liability, and the centralization of authority in a board of directors—had the potential of becoming a powerful tool of capitalism. Once set free by the liberalization of corporation laws after the Civil War, corporate entities quickly grew into quasi-governmental bodies. Sometimes these entities emerged as tyrannical and predatory, as in the case of the Rockefellers' Standard Oil Company. But other corporations were oligarchic, as was the case of Chicago's International Harvester Corporation, created in 1902. During the 1880s and 1890s McCormick's lead in the manufacture of threshing machines was violently contested by several smaller firms resulting in a chaotic and unprofitable "Harvester War." Finally, the Morgan Bank stepped in and negotiated a merger so that predictability and economic stability might be established.[63]

The model of the fair directors and Burnham was the second rather than the first, the corporation as a tool to establish order by combining separate interests into a great whole. In the case of architecture this meant the separation of design from execution and the restriction of design freedom by certain agreed limits. The problem was that there was now a chief executive—Burnham, Chief of Construction, in the case of the fair—who was not a designer, but rather part planner, part engineer, part businessman, all on his own unique model. Thus he escaped the squeeze affecting commercial architects by expanding laterally, by becoming a monopolist of architecture who could occupy his mind in organizing other men's fantasies.

The corporate model Burnham demonstrated at the fair could either be imposed on public architecture or set up in competition with it. Burnham pursued both paths. From 1894 to 1896 he served as president of the American Institute of Architects and pressed for the implementation of the Tarnsey Act of 1893, reorganizing the office of the Supervising Architect of the Treasury so that the post was only executive in nature, while design was placed in the hands of private architects selected by competition. He had to wait for complete satisfaction until his friends William McKinley and Theodore Roosevelt appointed his collaborator from the fair, Lyman Gage, Secretary of the Treasury. The system was put into effect, the result being a notable series of federal buildings by young artist-architects who found they could now make a career in this field.[64] Soon after, in 1901, Burnham arranged to the commission appointed to study the plan of Washington, D. C., resulting in the celebrated McMillan Committee report of 1902 and the subsequent rebuilding of the Capitol. In 1904 he visited the recently pacified Phillipines to replan Manila and to lay out a summer capital in the mountains at Baguio.[65]

Burnham also ventured into the field of reformed local government when in 1902-03 he served, together with John Merven Carrère and Arnold Brunner, on a commission to plan a monumental group of government buildings in Cleveland. But when it came to his native Chicago, he was more chary. In 1907 the Commercial Club—an association of the principal businessmen of the city—asked him to draft a plan for the transformation of the city. Aided by the Beaux-Arts trained designer Edward H. Bennett, whom he lured away from George B. Post's office in New York, the French architecture student Fernand Janin, and the renderer Jules Guérin, Burnham produced in 1909 the magnificent *Plan of Chicago*. More importantly, agitation was commenced at once to implement the plan. Bennett was appointed Consulting Architect to the Chicago Plan Commission (his salary and that of his staff paid for by the Commercial Club) and agitation for various specific improvements put afoot by the Commission chairman, Charles Wacker.[66] Propaganda on many levels was prepared and school children and neighborhood groups addressed. Project by project, parts of the great scheme came into being along the lakefront and North Michigan Avenue.

In speaking of the architects' restriction of their practice to commercial architecture, I have implied that this was chiefly to avoid the taint of corrupt local government. But commercial architecture also had a profoundly positive attraction as well. Burnham never let this side of his practice decline and when he commenced work on the Chicago Plan he ceased to accept planning commissions, referring inquiries on to his former assistant Bennett. In Burnham's hands the office building had become an urbanistic entity in itself, as is seen in his quarter-block square Railway Exchange (1903) and Peoples Gas (1910) buildings or most majestically in his full block Ellicott Square Building (figs. 44, 45) in Buffalo. This last project was too vast for a single client to finance, and Burnham had to organize himself and cajole prospective clients as if presenting a city plan. When built, it dominated Buffalo like a citadel of capitalism. Here Burnham solved the same problem that Adler and Sullivan had in their Schiller Building, but now by turning the building inside out—or better, outside in—for here an unbroken masonry cube rising straight from the sidewalk opens internally into a vast, balconied, glass-roofed piazza providing light and access from the center.[67]

The quality that was the newest and most stunning in the Court of Honor at the Columbian Exposition had been its regularity and closure. Olmsted had considered openness, irregularity, and pictur-

THE NINETEENTH CENTURY

Fig. 44 D. H. Burnham and Co., Architects. Exterior Elevation of Ellicott Square, 295 Main Street, Buffalo. 1892-96.

Fig. 45 D. H. Burnham and Co., Architects. Interior Court of Ellicott Square, 295 Main Street, Buffalo. 1892-96.

esque volumes of natural foliage to be the most important and therapeutic elements in decorative urbanism and so provided lagoons, an island, and banks of foliage around the fair buildings.[68] Root had sketched a varied, colorful ensemble at the Court of Honor, splashing with fountains, opening outward in broad arches, and upward with towers and pinnacles. But Burnham and his committee of architects created instead something very much like the courtyard of the Ellicott Square Building, complete with mechanical systems for movement (electric trains and wheel chairs) and electric lighting at night. Burnham replaced the therapy of wide nature with that of closed, regular architecture combined with mechanical amenity so that the whole world might become one great skyscraper, just as his friend Henry Blake Fuller implied in his *Cliff Dwellers*.

V.
Daniel Burnham was the great, unavoidable fact of Chicago architecture in 1900. To be an architect then was to position one's self in relation to him. One could join his organization; one could boldly but carefully seek a position from which to compete with him; one could flee to the suburbs. Burnham looms in every architect's autobiography of the time —as Paul Starrett's demanding but humane employer, "the handsomest man I ever saw";[69] as Sullivan's nemesis, admonishing, "It is not good policy to go much above the general level of intelligence";[70] as Frank Lloyd Wright's "Uncle Dan," tempting him like Mephistopheles in Edward C. Waller's library.[71] What, then, did architects maturing at the turn of the century do?

Wright was the brightest of that new generation. He had been Sullivan's chief draftsman for six years before being forced out because he had been doing work on his own. He had important experience. Charles Atwood died in 1895 and Burnham needed a new design partner. In a famous scene related by Wright in his *Autobiography*, a mutual friend, Waller, invited Wright and Burnham to dinner, then led them into the study and locked the door. Burnham proposed the partnership to Wright: "He would take care of my wife and children if I would go to Paris, four years at the Beaux-Arts. Then Rome— two years. Expenses all paid. Job with him when I came back." Wright turned him down.

One accepts this story readily because it reproduces the romantic paradigm of the young genius rejecting security for the sake of his art—like Keats, Byron, or Nietzsche. But was the acting out of a romantic scenario enough to motivate Wright on the spot, in Waller's study, in 1895? Wright was not yet established in 1895, and Burnham's offer presented two great advantages: first, it would have provided steady income exactly when Wright's growing family and rising tastes were carrying him into financial crisis; second, it was just the kind of opportunity a bright young architect had traditionally sought. It was, indeed, what Adler had offered Sullivan, twelve years his junior—"a contract for five years, beginning first of May. First year you one third, after that, even." It was what old Edward Burling had offered young Adler when they had gone into partnership in 1871. "Was this success as I had dreamed of it then," Wright wrote, "Right here, within my grasp?"

The comparison with Sullivan's partnership, however, brings out the most important difference in detail. Burnham's office organization was not so simple as Adler and Sullivan's. Burnham would be firmly in command. Furthermore, Wright would not be taken as he was: there was the stipulation of specialized training at the Ecole des Beaux-Arts and in Rome. Henry-Russell Hitchcock speculated that Burnham made the offer because Wright had proven himself the best classical designer in Chicago in his Charnley and Blossom houses and in his competition project for the Milwaukee library and museum.[72] It would, however, seem more logical that Burnham saw Wright as the best subordinate in the city because of his successful six years as a "pencil in the master's hand" at Adler and Sullivan. That is, Burnham made his offer to Wright because he believed him to be a blank sheet upon which six years of European education could inscribe what Burnham wished. The schooling was the thing at which Wright says he balked. "I've been too close to Mr. Sullivan. He has helped spoil the Beaux-Arts for me, or spoiled me for the Beaux-Arts, I guess I mean." A manner of design was not a choice but instead a moral necessity; being Sullivan's pencil was very different from being Burnham's. Wright perceived that employment with Burnham meant becoming a highly trained specialist, not a partner at all, but a cog in the corporate mechanism. "I know, Uncle Dan, you may be quite right but somehow it strikes on my heart like…jail."

Thus Wright refused to take the traditional step to success because of the way in which the profession had been transformed by Burnham and the fair. In 1895 he would have had his predecessor on Burnham's staff clearly in mind: Charles Atwood, an unassuming New Englander, a brilliant, intuitive designer, but a drug addict who finally committed suicide after being fired for incompetence.[73] Atwood was an extreme case, but his eventual successor as Burnham's design partner, Peirce Anderson, never established a clear individual personality. Burnham's friend and biographer Charles Moore depicts him rejecting a design because the detailing was from the draftsman's imagination rather than copied from an historical source: Burnham produced an architectural product of predictable quality, and in design, predictability lay in the reproduction of acknowledged models of good taste.[74]

Atwood's fate must indeed have seemed like "jail," or worse, but while the path that Sullivan had taken to success was now closed to Wright, a new route was simultaneously opening, through the suburbs. What Wright did after he had refused Burnham's offer, of course, was to become a house architect in suburban Oak Park (see fig. 46). His decision would seem parallel to that made by his friend Dwight Perkins, who left Burnham's office in 1894 after virtually running it during the construction of the fair, to set up practice as a domestic architect in Evanston. In 1907 Thomas E. Tallmadge similarly left Burnham for Evanston. They went, but they did not go far, as it turned out. The suburbs came into their own during the 1880s and 1890s, and Evanston was where one rubbed elbows socially with the most important clients, as well as with Burnham himself and William Holabird, who had moved there too. Indeed, Perkins, Tallmadge, Burnham, and Holabird collaborated in projects for civic betterment. The young men's relationship to the older men was still one of dependence, but a stronger one than that of Atwood or Anderson because of the trappings of social and professional equality. In fact, theirs was like the relationship Edward Bennett had established with Burnham in a different context. After his training at the Ecole des Beaux-Arts and in the office of George B. Post, Bennett had been employed specifically to design Burnham's West Point competition project (1902-03) and San Francisco plan (1904-05) and, finally, to superintend the Chicago Plan (1907-09). The latter project led to his appointment to the Chicago Plan Commission and to his founding a private practice, initially for city planning projects referred to him by Burnham.

The suburbs offered another attraction, however. It was the insulated environment of the new corporate elite, and the suburban architects were the well-born, well-educated men of social pretense. Clients could permit themselves a generosity in suburban building that they avoided in the Loop, and these earnest young men were ready to build slowly and expensively but well. Robert Twombley in his biography of Wright emphasized how during his years in Oak Park he was a perfect participant in the social scene, joining, entertaining, and hobnobbing with the best of his neighbors, conducting himself like Perkins or Tallmadge in Evanston.[75]

THE NINETEENTH CENTURY

Fig. 46 Frank Lloyd Wright, Architect. Ward Willitts House, 1445 Sheridan Road, Highland Park, Illinois. 1902.

By 1900, then, there was a clear division in Chicago architecture between the Loop and the suburbs, the latter ten miles from the former and still completely surrounded by market gardens. One was dominated by massive, efficient commercial buildings, the most notable by the firm of D. H. Burnham. The other consisted of a series of shady retreats, fantastic (as the dwelling-places of the rich always are) less in the ornamentation of their architecture than in the richness of their foliage, the breadth and orderliness of their streets, and the healthful openness of their habitation. But both were, as in New York, well connected by the elevated lines and commuter railroads. Unfortunately, one could no longer visit Chicago as Sullivan had in 1873 and choose what architect to work for by walking the streets. The Loop had been organized and regimented, while brilliance had been given a small territory of its own—the suburb—where it was tolerated privately and self-satisfyingly. For the first time what there was to "discover" in an American city was the traces of its old Victorian exuberance, when architects and their clients still tried to shout each other down on the sidewalks of the main streets. Sullivan's work was discovered and rediscovered, each time more sentimentally than before. Wright, however, in 1909 forsook even the suburb, outraging its social code by eloping with another man's wife, and retreated to Wisconsin to start the most profound and difficult part of his architectural career.[76]

VI.

Our optimistic confidence that order might be supportive of genius in Chicago architecture is based on the belief that Burnham was an architect-businessman in the same sense as Jenney, a hard-headed and somewhat piratical independent producing a better mousetrap. But I have tried to indicate how, as he led the fair to triumph in 1893, the situation was transformed and the individual—whether artist or monument—ceased to have value except as a part of a greater whole. Frank Lloyd Wright perceived this and—offered the opportunity any young American dreamed of in 1895—fled. Sullivan was too deeply enmeshed to escape; he railed at these developments in his *Kindergarten Chats* (1901-02), and, finally in 1924, he centered the last chapter of his *Autobiography* on the slaughter houses of the stockyards with the populace singing of democracy "as they are moved up the runways."[77]

New York and Chicago were the sites of the emergence of the great corporate architectural office just before the turn of the century. Architecture became part of the movement that had earlier produced the large, national firms in minerals, manufacturing, and transportation, themselves largely centered in these two cities. Chicago had the advantage of coming after New York, of perfecting New York's experiments and applying them in a newer, smaller, and less encumbered field. We can witness there with greater clarity and precision the forces affecting both cities. What we see is not really a story of unified devotion to genius in order and orderly genius in Chicago contrasting with a tale of mediocrity and chaos in New York. On the contrary, we watch in both cities the drama of art dealing with the great fact of American society at the end of the 19th century: the emergence of the corporate structure in all areas of endeavor.

Notes

Many people have been very kind helping me with the conceptualization and writing of this essay: Carl W. Condit, John Zukowsky, Robert Bruegmann, Neil Levine, and the staff of the Chicago Historical Society.

1. Siegfried Giedion, *Space, Time and Architecture*, 5th ed. (Cambridge, Mass., 1941), pp. 368ff. See also Carl W. Condit, *The Chicago School of Architecture: A History of Commercial and Public Building in the Chicago Area, 1875-1925* (Chicago, 1964).

2. Louis Sullivan, "The Tall Office Building Artistically Considered," *Lippincott's Magazine* 57 (Mar. 1896), pp. 403-09; reprinted in *Kindergarten Chats and Other Writings* (New York, 1947), pp. 202-03. Frank Lloyd Wright, "In the Cause of Architecture," *Architectural Record* 23 (Mar. 1908), p. 155.

3. Quoted in Harriet Monroe, *John Wellborn Root: A Study of his Life and Work* (Boston, 1896), pp. 136-37. For the original, see Paul Bourget, *Outre-Mer* (Paris, 1894), vol. 1, ch. 5.

4. Giedion (note 1), p. 374.

5. Homer Hoyt, *One Hundred Years of Land Values in Chicago* (Chicago, 1933).

6. Ibid., table 86, pp. 474-75.

7. Bourget (note 3); William H. Jordy and Ralph Coe, eds., *American Architecture and Other Writings by Montgomery Schuyler*, 2 vols. (Cambridge, Mass., 1961).

8. See Daniel Boorstin, *The Americans: The National Experience* (Chicago, 1965), pp. 124-34.

9. Hoyt (note 5), pp. 23-29, 42.

10. "A History of Chicago Architecture: The Recollections of John M. Van Osdel, Architect," *Inland Architect* (Aug. 1883), p. 89.

11. The publication *Industrial Chicago*, 6 vols. (Chicago, 1891-96), includes biographies of this first generation. See vol. 1, pp. 593-642.

12. On New York cast-iron architecture, see Daniel D. Badger, *Illustrations of Iron Architecture Made by the Architectural Iron Works of the City of New York* (New York, 1865) and James Bogardus, *Cast Iron Buildings: Their Construction and Advantages* (New York, 1856), both reprinted in *The Origins of Cast Iron Architecture in America* (New York, 1970).

13. Hoyt (note 5), table 86.

14. Theodore Turak, "William Le Baron Jenney: A Nineteenth Century Architect," (Ph.D. diss., University of Michigan, 1966). See also W. B. Mundie, *William Le Baron Jenney, 1832-1907* (Chicago, 1914).

15. Louis Sullivan, *The Autobiography of an Idea* (New York, 1924), pp. 203-04.

16. Mundie (note 14), p. 9.

17. Bertha W. Clark, *John Jenney of Plymouth and his Descendants to the Seventh Generation* (Boston, 1958).

18. This summary of Jenney's early career is in Mundie's pamphlet and is documented in part in Turak's thesis (see note 14), but still needs confirmation in many details.

19. Richard Schermerhorn, *Schermerhorn Geneology and Family Chronicles* (New York, 1914).

20. Hoyt (note 5), pp. 99-100.

21. Olmsted, Vaux and Company, *Preliminary Report upon the Proposed Suburban Village at Riverside, near Chicago* (New York, 1868); Riverside Improvement Company, *Riverside in 1871 with a Description of its Improvements* (Chicago [1871]).

22. Boorstin (note 8).

23. From an unidentified newspaper clipping in a scrapbook belonging to Jenney in the library of the Chicago Historical Society.

24. Mundie (note 14), n.p.

25. On Leiter, see Wayne Andrews, *The Battle for Chicago* (New York, 1946), pp. 28-29.

26. Hoyt (note 5), pp. 118ff.

27. See Sarah Bradford Landau, "The Tall Office Building Artistically Reconsidered: Arcaded Buildings of the New York School, c. 1870-1890," in *In Search of Modern Architecture: A Tribute to Henry-Russell Hitchcock*, ed. Helen Searing (New York, 1982), pp. 136-64.

28. *Industrial Chicago*, vol. 1, pp. 118ff.

29. *Memoir of General A. C. Ducat* (Chicago, 1897), pp. 65-67. Gerald Robert Larson of the University of Cincinnati will publish shortly an extensive study of the Home Insurance Building and its economic context.

30. *Engineering Record* (June 27, July 25, 1896); Frank A. Randall, *History of the Development of Building Construction in Chicago* (Urbana, 1949), pp. 105-07.

31. Frederick Baumann, *Improvements in the Construction of Tall Buildings* (Chicago, 1884).

32. I am grateful to Roula Geraniotis of the University of Illinois for this information.

33. Sullivan (note 15), pp. 312-13.

34. Mundie (note 14) lists the more successful draftsmen in Jenney's office. On Cudell, see Thomas E. Tallmadge, *Architecture in Old Chicago* (Chicago, 1941), pp. 118-19. On Edelmann, see D. D. Egbert and Paul E. Sprague, "In Search of John Edelmann, Architect and Anarchist," *American Institute of Architects Journal* 45 (Feb. 1966), pp. 35-41.

35. On Wight's varied career, see Sarah Bradford Landau, *P. B. Wight: Architect, Contractor, and Critic, 1838-1925* (Chicago, 1981).

36. See Sharon Darling, *Chicago Ceramics and Glass* (Chicago, 1979), pp. 161-65. On New York terracotta, see *A History of Real Estate, Building and Architecture in New York City During the Last Quarter of a Century* (New York, 1893; reprint, New York, 1967), pp. 509-28.

37. See Robert Bruegmann, "Holabird & Roche and Holabird & Root: The First Two Generations," *Chicago History* 9 (Fall 1980), pp. 130-65.

38. Jordy and Coe (note 7); see, for example, Schuyler's "Architecture in Chicago: Adler and Sullivan," in vol. 1, pp. 377-404.

39. *The Engineering Magazine* 1 (1891), pp. 185-202.

40. *The Engineering Magazine* 3 (1891-92), pp. 44-54, 637-47; 4 (1892-93), pp. 171-86; 7 (1894), pp. 717-30, 815-29; 12 (1897), pp. 643-49.

41. *The Engineering Magazine* 3 (1891-92), p. 300; 6 (1893-94), pp. 726-27, 892-93.

42. Barr Ferree, "The Modern Office Building," *Journal of the Franklin Institute* 141 (Jan.-Feb. 1896), pp. 47-140.

43. *The Engineering Magazine* 7 (1894), p. 160.

44. *Fraternity Temple: an Announcement to the Independent Order of Odd Fellows of Chicago...* (Chicago, 1891).

45. Donald Hoffmann, *The Architecture of John Wellborn Root* (Baltimore, 1973), pp. 19ff.

46. John W. Leonard, ed., *The Book of Chicagoans* (Chicago, 1905).

47. Earle Shultz and Walter Simmons, *Offices in the Sky* (Indianapolis and New York, 1959), p. 33.

48. See Paul Starrett, *Skyscrapers and the Men Who Build Them* (New York, 1928), and *Changing the Skyline* (New York, 1938). See also *Prominent Buildings Erected by the George A. Fuller Company* (Chicago, 1893, 1904, and 1910).

49. Henry Ericsson, *Sixty Years a Builder* (Chicago, 1942), p. 220.

50. Starrett, *Changing the Skyline*, p. 179.

51. This letterbook is in The Ryerson and Burnham Libraries of The Art Institute of Chicago.

52. Willard Connely, in *Louis Sullivan as He Lived* (New York, 1960), pp. 158ff., chronicled Sullivan's decline after his break with Adler in 1895.

53. Louis Sullivan, "Development of Building—II," *The Economist* 56 (July 1916), p. 40.

54. *A Half-Century of Chicago Building: A Practical Reference Guide* (Chicago, 1910), building code, pp. 135ff., especially those sections on pp. 229-31.

55. On Atwood, see A. L. Van Zanten, "The Marshall Field Annex and the New Urban Order of Daniel Burnham's Chicago," *Chicago History* 11 (Fall-Winter 1982), pp. 130-41. Mrs. Van Zanten completed before her death a more lengthy study of Atwood that I hope will soon be published.

56. Monroe (note 3), p. 82.

57. Starrett, *Changing the Skyline*, p. 53.

58. Sullivan (note 15), p. 314.

59. *Macmillan Encyclopedia of Architects*, s.v. "McKim, Mead, and White." See also Leland M. Roth, *The Architecture of McKim, Mead and White, 1879-1920: A Building List* (New York, 1978), xii-xlviii. In his most recent work on the firm (*McKim, Mead & White, Architects* [New York, 1983]), Roth discusses the atelier organization of the McKim, Mead and White firm, typical of architecture offices at the time, including Burnham and Root. This contrasts with the rise of the corporate hierarchy of D. H. Burnham and Co. See Roth (p. 5) citing Thomas Hines, *Burnham of Chicago* (Chicago, 1974), pp. 268-70

60. *Industrial Chicago* (note 11), vol. 1., pp. 150-52.

61. Ibid., pp. 613-14.

62. Ibid., pp. 606-07.

63. See Alan Trachtenberg, *The Incorporating of America* (New York, 1982), and Alfred D. Chandler, *The Visible Hand* (Cambridge, Mass., 1977), pp. 402ff.

64. See Hines (note 59), pp. 126ff.

65. Ibid., chs. 8-10.

66. See the exhibition catalogues published by The Art Institute of Chicago: *The Plan of Chicago, 1909-1979* (Chicago, 1979), which includes Sally Chappell, "Chicago Issues: The Enduring Power of a Plan," pp. 6-15, and Robert Bruegmann, "Burnham, Guérin and the City as Image," pp. 16-28; and Joan Draper, *Edward H. Bennett: Architect and City Planner, 1874-1954* (Chicago, 1982).

67. A. L. Van Zanten, "Charles Bowler Atwood and Daniel H. Burnham and Company," unpublished manuscript, 1982.

68. Frederick Law Olmsted, *Public Parks and the Enlargement of Towns* (Cambridge, Mass., 1870).

69. Starrett, *Changing the Skyline*, p. 23.

70. Sullivan (note 15), p. 316.

71. Frank Lloyd Wright, *An Autobiography* (New York, 1932), pp. 123ff.

72. Henry-Russell Hitchcock, "Frank Lloyd Wright and the Academic Tradition of the Early 1890's," *Journal of the Warburg and Courtauld Institutes* 7 (Jan.-June, 1944), pp. 46-63.

73. Van Zanten (note 55), p. 133.

74. Charles Moore, *Daniel H. Burnham: Architect, Planner of Cities* (Boston and New York, 1921), vol. 2, p. 166.

75. Robert Twombley, *Frank Lloyd Wright: His Life and Architecture* (New York, 1979), ch. 2.

76. Professor Neil Levine's current work is exploring Wright's crisis between 1909 and 1914.

77. Sullivan (note 15), pp. 304-08.

Sister Cities: Architecture and Planning in the Twentieth Century

Carol Herselle Krinsky

This exhibition celebrates American optimism of the late 19th and early 20th centuries, a time when the still-young nation was dynamic, inventive, powerful, and successful. Much of the energy was concentrated in our biggest cities—the centers of transportation, communication, finance, trade, research, and information resources. People's economic and spatial aspirations often go together, and in the great period of American ascendancy, despite intermittent declines, our buildings, ambitions, and airplanes all pushed upward. After all, New York had risen from its ashes in 1835 and Chicago had done the same in 1871. Art museums, philharmonic societies, parks, opera houses, universities, observatories, and zoological and botanical gardens combined aesthetic delights with science. At the same time, they helped to prepare citizens for the marriage of newly mature American art to American technology, a marriage that was consummated in the significant architectural achievements of the late 19th and early 20th centuries.

The spectacular age of the skyscraper—the dynamic city building that ceased at the time of the Great Depression—was predicated upon factors that were initially independent of architectural design. The country's ample mineral resources made high-rise construction in steel economically feasible, and they made possible the railways and ships (and their fuel) that brought ore to the refinery and thence to the shop and the construction site. The expanding economy absorbed an increasing labor force, much of it skilled in metalworking, masonry, and ornamental carving, and much of it desperate for any job, however unpleasant or dangerous it might be on a high-rise girder or in an underwater caisson. The changing nature of business—its enlargement, greater complexity, and specialization—required a volume of record-keeping that could only be accommodated in spacious offices. Private companies and burgeoning municipal agencies provided the infrastructure for further growth. The Sanitary and Ship Canal, built to provide Chicago with safe drinking water, and a supplementary New York water tunnel both opened at the turn of the century. Rapid transit rail services opened new areas to housing and small business while reinforcing the central business districts. Adjacent land was incorporated in New York and Chicago to rationalize municipal services and to keep prosperous taxpayers within city limits. There were new building regulations concerning fire safety, then housing, and, ultimately, comprehensive zoning (1916 in New York, 1923 in Chicago).

Abundant sources of inspiration suggested what our cities might be like if people with affirmative vision and managerial skills dared to shape them. The marvels of the world were assembled from Philadelphia to San Diego at exhibitions in specially designed fairgrounds, where they left vivid memories of well-managed, clean, intelligently planned, and handsome urban environments. The White City of Chicago, the World's Columbian Exposition of 1893, was radiant with white palaces that dazzled the public at night thanks to electric lights. The 1901-02 plans for the redevelopment of Washington, D. C.—a fairground made permanent—inspired the members of the Merchants Club (and, later, the Commercial Club) in Chicago. They had been meeting with architects and government officials since the close of the 1893 fair to plan for a more orderly city, one that would rival Washington and exceed New York in civic beauty. Even school children were exposed to civics books, some, such as W. D. Moody's *Wacker's Manual of the Plan of Chicago* (1911), modeled on a handbook devised in connection with the 1909 Chicago Plan that was published under the auspices of the Commercial Club. In both the Chicago Plan and *Wacker's Manual*, schemes for urban beautification and the improvement of transportation systems (see cats. 11, 12) were presented as issues that were as important to the citizenry as public health and sanitation.

Both Chicago and New York, as the nation's premier metropolitan centers, were filled with the entrepreneurs, merchants, clerks, intellectuals, and laborers whose activities created the heady atmosphere, conducive to great building, that was found in America at the turn of the century. Many of the architectural achievements in both cities therefore reveal similar ambitions. The citizens (and architects) of both faced similar problems and solved them with similar artistic forms. But generally comparable circumstances cannot explain the outcome of a specific commission and architectural program, nor can they overcome some fundamental differences in the structures of the two metropolises. A brief examination may help to remind us why the two cities, for all their common features, retain their own visual character.

I.
In addition to natural similarities among businessmen and civic leaders in both cities, there were connections established by interlocking directorates, families, and friendships. Architects traveled between the cities then as some do today. George B. Post, the innovative designer of civic, commercial, and institutional buildings in New York (see cats.

47, 53, 55), was responsible for the Manufacturers' Building at the 1893 fair. The firm of McKim, Mead and White of New York designed the fair's Agricultural Building. In Chicago, they also designed houses for the McCormick-Patterson newspaper magnates of the *Chicago Tribune* (cat. 3) and for Bryan Lathrop (fig. 9; cats. 27, 28). Charles F. McKim knew Daniel H. Burnham of Chicago well, having served with him on the Capital Park Commission that replanned Washington, D.C. Burnham's firm designed one of New York's most famous buildings, the Flatiron (fig. 18; cat. 4; formerly the Fuller Building). Burnham also designed the impressive, but less famous, Wanamaker Annex (1903) at Broadway and 8th Street. Ernest R. Graham, Burnham's partner and successor, designed the Equitable Building (fig. 59). Later, the firm of Graham, Anderson, Probst and White designed the Chase National Bank Building (fig. 47). Louis Sullivan is represented in New York by the Bayard-Condict Building (fig. 2) a few blocks south of the Wanamaker Annex.

Frank Lloyd Wright, who worked for a time in Sullivan's firm, proposed comparable apartment tower designs in 1929 for both Chicago and New York. Tenants were to inhabit two-story dwellings with glass-walled living rooms in buildings with unconventional prismatic forms expressing modernity. They were intended for an unspecified site in Chicago, and for the churchyard and adjacent lots beside St. Mark's-in-the-Bouwerie in New York, where the minister hoped to erect housing that would support his church financially. While the stock market crash put an end to those plans, Wright offered other housing proposals to New York in 1953, in the form of an exhibition house erected on the site of his later Guggenheim Museum. There, visitors could see how much convenience might be possible in a 1,700-square-foot, two-bedroom house, 12 feet high, intended for virtually any American site outside a city center.[1]

The most conspicuous intercity practitioner between the World Wars was Raymond Hood, who in 1922 developed the winning design for the Chicago Tribune Tower competition with New York architect John Mead Howells (see cat. 62). From then on, Hood worked in both cities, though principally in New York. For Chicago, in conjunction with Holabird and Root and Voorhees, Gmelin and Walker, he

Fig. 47 Graham, Anderson, Probst and White, Architects. Chase National Bank Building, New York. 1928.

Fig. 48 Joseph Urban, Architect. The New School for Social Research, 66 West 12th Street, New York. 1930.

proposed plans in 1927-29 for the development of the tract of land at the mouth of the Chicago River that is now Illinois Center (cat. 14); he also collaborated on the 1933 Century of Progress Exposition. One of the leading fair planners was Harvey Wiley Corbett, like Hood a migrant to New York. Corbett's firm collaborated with Hood's on the design of Rockefeller Center (fig. 72), while the fair plans were underway. The man in charge of the color scheme at the fair was Joseph Urban, a stage and building designer who, although not a licensed architect, designed the New School for Social Research (fig. 48) and the International Magazine Building in New York (1928; later the Hearst Building). Somewhat less interesting architects, like the New York firm of Sloan and Robertson, worked for less imaginative developers, including the Fred F. French Company and the Irwin Chanin Company, who provided a background of massive skyscrapers with attractive and stylish decorations much as the Burnham Brothers and Thielbar and Fugard did in Chicago.

Since the revival of building after the Second World War, architects have often designed buildings for both cities. The firm of Skidmore, Owings and Merrill—the first two partners had been recruited by Hood to work on the 1933 fair—became internationally famous with Lever House (fig. 49) in New York, designed by Gordon Bunshaft, and with the Inland Steel Building in Chicago (fig. 50; cat. 63), by Bruce J. Graham, with the Chase Manhattan Bank headquarters in New York (1957-60) following closely afterward. SOM's Chicago and New York offices were established in 1936. Ludwig Mies van der Rohe, while active on many projects in Chicago, where his influence was profound, designed the famous Seagram Building in New York with Philip Johnson, Kahn and Jacobs. Lever House and the Seagram Building, two glass-sheathed boxes beside open plazas, inspired the comprehensive New York zoning changes of 1961 that allowed builders to combine public plazas with profitable height. The Tishman Construction company now designs and builds office towers in both cities, sometimes under Mies's inspiration as transmitted by the Skidmore firm (e.g., Gateway Center, 1963-65, 1967-69, 1969-70). William Lescaze, a designer of houses and office buildings in New York, worked with the Chicago firm of A. Epstein and Sons on the Borg-Warner Building (1957-58). Even younger and smaller firms, such as Kohn, Pedersen and Fox of New York and Scott Himmel and Darcy Bonner of Chicago, have received commissions in both cities, and architects in both cities travel between the two in order to serve on juries, to consult, and to teach.

Fig. 49 Gordon Bunshaft of Skidmore, Owings and Merrill, Architects. Lever House, 390 Park Avenue, New York. 1947-52.

Fig. 50 Bruce J. Graham of Skidmore, Owings and Merrill, Architects. Inland Steel Building, 30 West Monroe Street, Chicago. 1955-57.

Some of the intercity travel stems from a client's desire to employ a specialist or a currently fashionable or inventive architect. Their proficiency explains the employment in both cities of Frederick Law Olmsted to design parks, or, later, of Rapp and Rapp and John Eberson to design theaters. It also accounts for the participation of several New York architects at the Century of Progress (see cats. 74, 75). When the fair was in its preparatory stages, Hood and Corbett were the only architects of stature in America who were involved on a large, multiple building project, and their Rockefeller Center, like the fair, had to be attractive to appeal to prospective customers and tenants in the depths of the Depression.

Clients, too, sometimes had interests in both cities. The New York Central and Pennsylvania railroads brought their trains into Chicago stations and had a voice in their design. John D. Rockefeller, who paid for the construction of Riverside Church in New York, also donated funds for a chapel at the University of Chicago. But even when the clients were not identical, they often had similar goals, which sometimes led a corporate or city official in one place to borrow ideas from the other.

We can see this clearly in late 19th- and early 20th-century railroad buildings. Because of the large amount of land (preferably flat and low-lying) needed for tracks and a station, and the noxiousness of the smoke and steam emitted by steam engines, railroad stations were originally located at city edges, where land was cheapest. When the first Grand Central Terminal was built in New York (cat. 8), it was at the northern edge of the city's development, while several railway companies' freight lines hugged the Hudson shoreline much as they did the river and lakefront in Chicago. By the turn of the century, the Grand Central Terminal at 42nd Street was almost surrounded by trolley lines, hotels, gentlemen's clubs, and office buildings, and an elevated railway ran nearby. Between 1901 and 1903, the LaSalle Street Station at Van Buren Street in Chicago was rebuilt by architects Charles Frost and Alfred Granger (who were related to the railway owner) and engineers Edward and Ralph Shankland.[2] They and their client understood the attractiveness of a station with immediate access to the Loop elevated railway, a convenience no earlier Chicago station had enjoyed. They also appreciated the financial benefits of connecting an office building with the headhouse. New York's Pennsylvania Station (McKim, Mead and White, 1902-10) included a subway line that ran under the tracks to the railroad tunnel beneath the Hudson River; a station for the Long Island Railroad; tunnels leading to two nearby hotels; and a headhouse, track shelter, and a huge post office built on the air rights. Immediately afterward, Grand Central Terminal was rebuilt (fig. 51). The architects—first Reed and Stem, later Warren and Wetmore—provided for the crossing of new subway lines under the rail tracks, access to trolley lines, an elevated road around the headhouse, the development of new office buildings and hotels on railroad property and air rights, and the construction of an office building over the tracks directly north of the headhouse. The transportation interchange at Grand Central allowed the New York Central Railroad company to become the primary developer of the midtown business district. In turn, the incipient success of the projects in New York must have inspired Daniel Burnham and the other members of the Chicago Plan team.[3] Their recommendations for consolidating railroad stations and terminal facilities in Chicago (see cat. 12) appeared just at the time when the Chicago and North Western Station (1906-11) was being built with exceptional facilities, sufficient for handling a volume of traffic that could have satisfied New York's needs.[4]

In New York the development of Grand Central Terminal and Pennsylvania Station solved several problems.[5] Since 1891, the officials of the Pennsylvania Railroad and of its subsidiary Long Island Railroad had been interested in running trains through tunnels under the Hudson and East rivers, respectively, in order to bring passengers into Manhattan without having them transfer to ferries. The practicability of electric train travel, which was vital to passage through an underwater tunnel, had been demonstrated for light railways in London's City and South London Railway (1887-90) and for standard service in the Belt Railroad tunnel of the Baltimore and Ohio lines (1895), while the Gare d'Orsay in

Fig. 51 Reed and Stem, and Warren and Wetmore, Associate Architects. Grand Central Terminal, 42nd Street and Vanderbilt Avenue, New York. 1903-13.

Paris proved the feasibility of an entire electrified rail terminal (1897-1900). The Pennsylvania may have been pushed into action when the North Jersey Street Railway Company announced in the autumn of 1901 that it planned to operate its vehicles through tunnels under the Hudson that would complete its run from Philadelphia to Manhattan. Perhaps to stymie these potential rivals, the Pennsylvania announced plans for tunnel trains and a new station in December of the same year. In the following month, two steam-powered trains collided in a tunnel, a contributory cause being obscured vision. The New York state legislature decided in 1903 that railway companies would have to prevent such accidents from recurring by providing smoke-free conditions in train tunnels after July 1, 1908. To comply, the New York Central and its affiliates had to electrify the railway lines south of 96th Street, which were partly covered, and to use electric traction motors in tunnels.

During the same decade, a network of 62 miles of tunnels was being built in Chicago's Loop area, at first to hold telephone and telegraph cables and then, after 1903, to contain tracks for small electric trains that carried freight to stores, offices, storage facilities, railway stations, and freight terminals, and rubbish to disposal vehicles and dumping sites.[6] The function of this system, of course, was different from that of the passenger-oriented network in New York, but the principle of a multipurpose, multi-layer, coordinated transportation and building development was analogous. A comparable state of engineering and planning served economic needs in both cities.

From an aesthetic point of view, there were other similarities between railroad designs in both cities. Grand Central Terminal and North Western station were both products of the age of grandiose Beaux-Arts classicism, exhibiting the maximum attainable symmetry in planning, with vast halls, soaring semi-circular arches, and the application of columns and allegorical statues. In addition, each building employed vaults introduced by Rafael Guastavino y Esposito[7]—thin rectangular terracotta tiles laid in an interlocked pattern, with mortar constituting half the total mass (see fig. 52). These vaults can be erected without the formwork that is usually required, and less of this vaulting by weight can carry loads as heavy as those borne by other types of vaulting. Because the attractive design of the tiles is produced directly by the method of their construction, their appearance is unrelated to the classicistic design of the exterior and main reception spaces. In separating utilitarian from rhetorical forms, these

Fig. 52 Frost and Granger, Architects. Ground Floor Ticket Office, Chicago and North Western Station, Madison Street between Canal and Clinton Streets, Chicago. 1906-11.

Fig. 53 Graham, Anderson, Probst and White, Architects. Union Station, Canal Street between Adams Street and Jackson Boulevard, Chicago. 1924-25.

SISTER CITIES

two stations and other contemporary ones typified the work of a generation that refused to elevate construction materials into a conscious aesthetic for the outsides and main public areas of civic or elegant private buildings.

The same classicistic aesthetic governed the exterior design by Graham, Anderson, Probst and White of Union Station in Chicago (fig. 53), which, although not opened until 1925, had been proposed in the Chicago Plan of 1909 and initiated two years later.[8] The exterior is a ponderous composition in two parts, one a low concourse and the other a headhouse with an office building above it. The concourse is an austere structure on the outside, with a taller central section and low wings. Almost all of the exterior surface is stone, and the window openings are small except at the riverfront where a high arch opens, interrupted by two heavy columns and a cornice above them that separates the curve of the arch from its lower opening. The headhouse features a Roman Doric portico below the office block. Earlier designs for the station proposed a more festive classical style and a clerestory with thermal windows rising behind the ground floor colonnade. The result would have been a station closely resembling Pennsylvania Station (fig. 54) in New York, a similarity which would have been understandable since the Pennsylvania owned half the stock in the Union Station company. (The design had to be changed when an office was placed over the headhouse, and the greater simplicity of the exterior may have been dictated by cost considerations, or by a developing taste for simpler surfaces.) The interior of the concourse was a five-aisled basilica divided by slender steel latticework piers that held glass barrel vaults (fig. 55). This concourse was a revised version of the one at Pennsylvania Station.

Connections between railway lines and buildings other than freight and passenger stations had been attempted in both cities from the late 19th century. The Bush Terminal in Brooklyn, begun in the 1890s, is a complex of piers, railroad sidings, warehouses, and factories on 200 acres of waterfront property. In 1891, the Central Stores/Terminal Warehouse Company buildings in New York were situated near the Lehigh Valley Railroad freight terminal, and warehouse facilities—usually on a smaller scale—were obvious and suitable neighbors to freight stations everywhere. In Chicago, the Central Manufacturing District (1902-10) was a complex of manufacturing and storage facilities located on 300 acres along railway lines; it required the construction not just of buildings but also of streets, sewers, and utilities as if it were an entire new town.[9] In New York, one

Fig. 54 McKim, Mead and White, Architects. Waiting Room, Pennsylvania Station, New York. 1910 (now demolished).

Fig. 55 Graham, Anderson, Probst and White, Architects. Main Waiting Room, Union Station, Canal Street between Adams Street and Jackson Boulevard, Chicago. 1924-25.

early 20th-century example of ingenious coordination of facilities is the connection of the Hudson and Manhattan Railroad Company's tube train line from New Jersey to a passage leading to the Dey Street subway station, with all the tunnels running underneath the massive 22-story Cortlandt and Fulton buildings (Clinton and Russell, architects; George A. Fuller Co., builders and engineers), which were connected by a bridge.[10] When finished in 1908, they were the world's largest office buildings in terms of square footage. They yielded in 1969 to the current version of a coordinated building and transportation facility, the World Trade Center, which held the record for a while as the world's tallest buildings.

Between the World Wars, another immense structure in New York was ingeniously tied into the railway network—the Starrett-Lehigh Building, facing the Hudson River in the block bounded by 26th and 27th streets. Built in 1931 to the design of Russell G. and Walter M. Cory with Yasuo Matsui, this structure emphasized the horizontality of the superimposed floors intended for firms which manufactured, displayed, stored, repacked, and distributed merchandise that arrived and left by rail and ship.[11] The Starrett-Lehigh was located at this marginal site because only west of Eighth Avenue did the zoning rules allow industrial activity, and here the building stood adjacent to the New York Central Railroad freight tracks over the former Lehigh Valley terminal. Railway cars could be diverted to the building's own rail yard, where trucks could be brought by elevators to the upper stories for convenient and secure unloading on a company's own floor.

In the same years, the Chicago Merchandise Mart (fig. 56) was rising over the air rights of the North Western Railroad.[12] Like the Starrett-Lehigh Building, it emphasized extensive and uninterrupted floor capacity rather than height, and it also had more than one purpose, as it was to have been both the headquarters of the wholesale division of Marshall Field and Company and the North Western freight terminal for shipments less than a carload in size. When it was built by Alfred Shaw of Graham, Anderson, Probst and White, its four million square feet made it the largest building in the world.

With certain differences, the Starrett-Lehigh Building and the Merchandise Mart employed similar approaches to the expression of function and to construction on a monumental scale. Both were utilitarian buildings, not the headquarters of famous corporations such as Woolworth or Wrigley, and it was therefore possible for the architects to use a style that revealed function and structure. The building in New York was especially explicit about these matters. For manufacturing and storage, it

Fig. 56 Graham, Anderson, Probst and White, Architects. Merchandise Mart, North bank of the Chicago River between Wells and Orleans Streets, Chicago. 1923-30.

needed wide floors interrupted by as few vertical supports as possible. All but the lowest three stories, which are steel-framed, are cantilevered concrete slabs with some verticals thereby eliminated from the interior. The vast floors stretch out and sweep around corners. Only the taller, steel-framed service core near the center emphasizes verticality; this is structurally expressive because only there and on the bottom three floors do verticals appear on the building's exterior. The succession of huge floors can be seen outside as light-colored horizontal bands of concrete; brick parapets under ribbon windows add other horizontal lines (see fig. 57). The varied colors and textures and the polygonal corners that look curved add graceful elements, making the building handsome as well as functional.

The Merchandise Mart in more traditional massing articulates its center by a truncated tower and terminates in slightly salient low, towerlike bays with canted corners. It has a two-story base, a shaft of identical floors, and a kind of capital area composed of setback floors that were prompted by Chicago's 1923 zoning rules. The exterior design nevertheless expresses a steel column and girder framing, with the vertical columns emphasized. An even grid on a building of this size in a central location would have been even duller as an urban accent than the facade that was used.

Despite the fact that they were useful and sometimes brilliantly integrated with the urban fabric, railroad tracks added nothing to the beauty and self-esteem of a city. Tracks blighted the west side waterfront of New York and the lake and river shores of Chicago. They interrupted streets in central Chicago, and crosstown traffic north of Grand Central had to be carried over the tracks on bridges that were disguised as streets. On the west side of Manhattan, trains at grade level caused so many accidents—in spite of the horseman who rode ahead of trains waving a red warning flag[13]—that these railway tracks began to be elevated in 1929. Elevated tracks brought darkness and lower real estate values to the streets below; consequently, some of the low-income tenements in New York and the unattractive shops in Chicago's Loop lay along them (fig. 58).[14] Older elevated trains were not electrified in New York until 1902, and in the preceding 24 years, smoke and steam bathed the tenements on Second, Third, Sixth, and Ninth avenues. Not until the els were removed, and in some locations not for years thereafter, were those streets endowed with more costly or elegant buildings.

SISTER CITIES

Fig. 57 Russell G. and Walter M. Cory, Architects, with Yasuo Matsui, Associate Architect. Starrett-Lehigh Building, West 26th Street between Eleventh and Twelfth Avenues, New York. 1931.

Fig. 58 Elevated tracks at Franklin and Lake Streets, Chicago.

One solution to the problem of visible tracks was the air rights park, an idea related to that of air rights buildings. The World's Columbian Exposition had developed waterfront land as a park. Bridges over rail tracks along the lakefront made the fairgrounds accessible from the west. While the fair was being planned, a committee appointed in 1891 by the New York City Board of Estimate recommended a "two-level design on reclaimed land between the [west side railroad] tracks and the river. [O]n the lower level, there would be a road for commercial traffic. On the higher level,...a wide road for pleasure vehicles and a 50-foot grand equestrian promenade."[15] In the influential 1909 Chicago Plan, Daniel Burnham had proposed creating waterfront parks by landfill techniques. These parks were to be reached by bridges over the tracks like those at the 1893 fair. Because many of Chicago's trains were not electrified until the 1950s, creating a lid over the steam-clouded tracks would have been impossible; but in anticipation of electrification, Burnham's Chicago Plan showed some covered tracks (see cat. 12). Covering tracks and integrating the lid with a waterfront landfill park was actually initiated in New York in 1934, when Robert Moses, the prodigious builder who was then Commissioner of the New York City Parks Department, obtained funding to execute his plans for the Hudson riverfront from 72nd to 125th streets. Perhaps taking a cue from the Burnham plan, Moses covered the rail tracks with the Henry Hudson Parkway, which has planted areas on either side and an underpass to a boat basin at 79th Street. Above 83rd Street, the parkway hugs the riverfront for much of its course, as does the drive along the shore of Lake Michigan (1917-39), likewise bounded by a parkland chain created largely of landfill (1911-33). South of 72nd Street, the parkway forms part of an elevated ring road around Manhattan. Older streets under the raised portions create a low-speed local traffic path. This two-level route, other streets under elevated rail lines, and the raising of Park Avenue around Grand Central Terminal are the closest parallels in New York to Chicago's Wacker Drive, which was also developed as part of the 1909 plan (first part completed 1925-26). Designs for this multilevel construction along the Chicago River envisioned streetcar tunnels below a 135-foot-wide roadway for heavy commercial vehicles that served warehouses and industrial and terminal facilities, and above it all, a 110-foot-wide road for general traffic that would be bordered by pedestrian promenades.

In other significant ways, Chicago and New York provided a comparable background for building. The expression of verticality in tall structures, especially offices, was a matter of concern to thoughtful architects in both cities. Sarah Bradford Landau has recently demonstrated that New York architects—in advance of their contemporaries in Chicago—experimented with facade designs that linked several stories of windows under one tall arch and that used arcading to organize pier and window rhythms.[16] Architects in Chicago led the way in expressing skeletal steel structure, at least on the facades of certain types of buildings, primarily speculative office towers, lofts, and department stores. It is true that since 1848 builders of cast-iron buildings (see cat. 42) in New York had provided models for a spare esthetic derived from construction techniques, but Chicago architects developed satisfying new ways to express structure and applied their ideas to tall buildings. After an initial period of innovation, probably stimulated by the advent of the tall office building that maximized profitable use of a site, many architects in both cities found ways to cloak their steel-framed buildings in cladding that suggested traditional monumental architecture (see cats. 54, 55) Architect John A. Holabird, a descendant of William Holabird, one of the innovators of structural expression, recently summarized three reasons for the abandonment of the innovative designing. In doing so, he recalled the distinction made between utilitarian and other buildings:

> There was a feeling at that time if you left the building completely unadorned—well, no one could face that. You did that for warehouses, but not for downtown buildings. Later on, firms like my grandfather's did warehouses and on those they didn't put any decoration at all. Some people think those are the most beautiful and purest expression of the Chicago School. But I'm sure the clients of these warehouses told the architects to leave out anything beautiful and to make it *cheap*.

He also reminded us of the disadvantages of large windows in that period. The architect John Wellborn Root, Jr., had told him

> that the real problem was... that because of these big glass areas [the buildings] were difficult to keep comfortable. The glazing was just single pane.[17]

Rooms inside these buildings, therefore, were hot in summer and cold in winter. Nevertheless, natural light, which was cheaper than gaslight and without risk of fire, maintained its appeal until "electric light came in, [and] they began to cut down the window size... because it was more convenient and more comfortable."[18] This change led to surfaces with more masonry, and the surfaces required some artistic treatment rather than only minimal cladding for the small amount of steel which remained next to wide windows. During and after the World's Columbian Exposition, according to Holabird, "people wanted to get the best." "Best" at that time meant imitating the fair's buildings, or the city's newly enlarged art museums, libraries, and railway station headhouses, which had never abandoned historicist styles. "[I]n those days the New York and Boston architects were the experts" and those experts were building the masonry-clad neoclassical and neo-Gothic public and institutional buildings which served as models for the style of commercial buildings.

The rapid growth of high-rise construction was related to business consolidation and to the growth of firms of huge size which demanded contiguous office spaces. This meant, in many cases, a new corporate headquarters in a single high-rise building (see cats. 54, 56). This type of building required the perfection of caisson construction (which opened previously unsuitable moist lands to heavy construction), the perfection of the steel frame, elevators of increased speed, high-pressure water systems for sanitary and drinking water on all floors, and the widespread use of electric lighting that allowed a workplace 30 feet from a window to be better and more safely lit than gaslit interiors had been.

The increased number and size of central-city buildings created a situation of threatening density in both Chicago and New York. It threatened the general public with congested transit facilities and streets. People worried about how quickly they could escape from high floors of burning buildings, or how many workers could run along the crowded sidewalks once they escaped. New Yorkers wondered how much more traffic could move on lower Manhattan's narrow streets. The incidence of tuberculosis was thought to increase in dark places, and sick leaves were more often taken by those who worked in dark offices. The situation threatened real estate owners who feared that their own buildings would lose light and air to new tall buildings next door, or that their own high-rises would soon be overshadowed, literally and aesthetically. In New York, as early as 1916, artificial lighting was needed at noon in midsummer in almost all the street-front rooms in offices on Exchange Place, where buildings were 11 to 22 stories high.[19]

The inefficiency of long commuting time, even with new trains and subways, and the congestion of some areas while open land abounded elsewhere stimulated thoughts about more rational and economical use of space in both cities. In New York in 1908, an exhibition at the American Museum of Natural History demonstrated to the public the wisdom of urban planning, and another display the following year at a midtown armory illustrated remedies developed in parts of the United States, some of its territories, and in England, Scotland, and Germany. A Heights of Buildings Commission was established in 1908 to consider remedies for the city's new congestion.

At about the same time, the Chicago Plan of 1909 proposed buildings of about 13 stories on grand boulevards, even though steel framing made it possible to build economically and beautifully at much greater heights. If it seems odd that Burnham and his associates repudiated Chicago's high-rise technology, the explanation may be that tall and structurally expressive buildings seemed suited to the utility-minded raw young Chicago of the immediate post-fire years, but not to the mature, well-planned City Beautiful of a generation later. In the end, of course, the plan did nothing to halt the development of huge buildings in the Loop.

A catalyst to building regulation in New York was provided by the construction of the Equitable Building (fig. 59) on Broadway between Pine and Cedar streets. It occasioned a loud outcry from real estate owners in lower Manhattan who feared the incursion of other similar buildings and a chaotic alteration of land values. In 1912 there was already a surfeit of vacant office space nearby.[20] The architect of the Equitable Building, Ernest Graham of Chicago, designed 1,200,000 square feet of floor space on a site slightly smaller than one acre. The 38-story structure cast a noontime shadow four blocks long, blocked ventilation on Thames Street, dumped at least 13,000 workers onto nearby sidewalks and transit facilities, and presented a problem for firefighters.[21] Its size was terrifying because in 1913 there were only 51 buildings in the whole city over 20 stories high, and only 9 of these were taller than 30 stories.[22]

The solution—or rather, partial solution—adopted was zoning: the division of cities into districts where certain types of buildings and activities were permitted, and where buildings of certain heights were allowed.[23] This combination of regulations was unprecedented in the United States when New York's rules took effect in 1916. According to these regulations, new buildings on specified streets in lower Manhattan and midtown business areas could rise straight up from the sidewalk to a point two-and-a-half times the street width. An imaginary

SISTER CITIES

Fig. 59 Ernest Graham of Graham, Anderson, Probst and White, Architects. Equitable Building, 120 Broadway, New York. 1912-15.

line would then be drawn from the center of the street to the cornice at that height. This diagonal, when projected into the lot, created a "sky exposure plane" under which all other cornices would have to fit. Rules governing setbacks on sides other than the street front established relationships between the lowest cornice and permissible towers: for example, when a building stepped back to cover only a quarter of a lot, a tower was allowed to reach as high as the building owner desired. Structures on narrow streets, on the interior lots of a block, or in other parts of the city, however, were often restricted to first cornice heights of one or one-and-a-half times the street width.

In Chicago there were few restrictions on land use and exploitation. In 1913 the governor of Illinois had vetoed a bill to allow cities to keep industrial facilities out of residential neighborhoods.[24] In 1918, however, an architects' committee including Holabird and Roche, Andrew Rebori, and Howard Van Doren Shaw proposed that heights be limited and that architectural standards be introduced on the newly improved North Michigan Avenue. A maximum building height of 260 feet above grade was, in fact, in force in central Chicago until 1923, when a new building regulation modeled in part on New York's zoning resolution allowed additions if they did not exceed a quarter of the lot area and a sixth of the building's volume, and if the building envelope was set back one foot in ten from lines of adjacent property. Towers above the 260-foot line, which earlier could not have been occupied, were now opened to office tenants.[25] Zoning districts set aside 23 percent of the city's land for industrial and manufacturing use, 14 percent for commercial use, and only 3 percent for single-family housing, although at that time industrial and single-family housing each occupied 12 percent of the city's land. The zoning rules favored intensive use of land by allocating 19 percent for two-family and 5 percent for multiple-family and apartment housing,[26] even though most Americans prefer single-family housing.[27] The rules left 75 percent of the land then used for such housing vulnerable to non-residential encroachment, with the possibility for sudden, drastic changes in property values. This plan was related to the idea of property taxation based on "highest and best" land use—a real estate term usually meaning most intensive—a notion that has fostered overbuilding in both Chicago and New York.

Zoning affected the future of both cities in other important ways. It seemed to be a practical substitute for city planning and doubtless forestalled the study of more issues besides height and land use. It encouraged developers to erect buildings up to the bulk limits of a site and to devise new architectural forms to accommodate the zoning regulations. It confirmed the high land values in the commercial zones, as well as the low values in unrestricted zones. This fixing of vastly different land values contributed to colossal overbuilding in some districts and absurd underdevelopment a few blocks away, as happened in Manhattan where an unrestricted zone began west of Eighth Avenue. New York's zoning rules would have allowed working space for three hundred million people if the areas zoned for commerce and manufacturing had been fully built up! Into those areas came hundreds of thousands of commuters each day, but hardly anyone could live in the vicinity. Only recently have city planners concerned themselves with implementing the "24-hour city" by letting people live in manufacturing zones, allowing multiple-use buildings, and assisting in the conversion of under-used office buildings to residences. These changes alter a situation in which parts of a city were shut down over the weekend—over 28 percent of the week.

The zoning rules also altered the visual appearance of cities. The standard first cornice height eventually lent visual unity to many streets, although technical and economic factors had already made many street fronts into solid phalanxes of similar and equally tall structures; the factors included the attainable speed of elevators and the lengths of their cables and mechanisms, fire safety codes, and cost-benefit analyses that made many buildings stop where the elevator shafts did. In their effect on the front and back of all buildings—and on a building's sides on certain sites—the setback provisions forced architects to design in three dimensions. Many earlier buildings had been mere boxes with planar facades pasted on.

The effects of zoning, good and bad, were not immediately visible in New York because high-rise building did not occur at a substantial level for half a decade after 1916. The city officials in Chicago may have delayed instituting zoning until 1923 because they wanted to see how the New York rules would work. Perhaps, too, there seemed to be less urgency to institute zoning in Chicago because a loftier vision (of uniform cornice lines) had already been offered in the 1909 plan.

Indeed, the Plan of Chicago remained a source of inspiration to city planners, to administrators of streets, traffic, rail facilities, parks, and public buildings, until the Second World War. It discussed the need for new traffic arteries, a matter that became ever more pressing, and it presented the benefits of coordinating railway facilities. The nature and location of buildings for the city, state, county, and federal governments were examined. The plan outlined the benefits to public health and happiness to be gained from parks, recreation areas, and neighborhood playgrounds. It became the officially adopted municipal plan in 1917, and, as it included facilities to be constructed up to 60 miles from the Loop, it was almost a regional plan in geographic extension. The plan was far-sighted in its discussions, but it neglected some absolutely critical matters, notably slums and housing for the poor, which took up only a few sentences of the large book.

Nevertheless, the Chicago Plan was one of the principal sources for the Regional Plan of New York and New Jersey, which was conceived in 1921 by Charles D. Norton, an official of the Russell Sage Foundation, which published the Plan's proposals from 1927 to 1931.[28] Like the Chicago Plan, this was the work of a private group led by acknowledged experts in planning, transportation, and architecture. Not surprisingly, many of the members of New York's planning committee had served on Chicago's. The New York area plan expressed a need for lower densities through dispersal and the creation of new industrial, business, and retailing areas (entailing conflict with the predictable results of the zoning resolution, which encouraged building to the maximum permissible density); proposed that residential areas be located near industrial workplaces in outlying areas; outlined better transportation facilities (which simply would manage central-city congestion better, not abolish it) (see fig. 60); and presented measures for urban beautification. This plan did not question the fundamental economic principles that had fostered the current congestion, probably because its sponsors, like those in Chicago, were primarily concerned with removing physical impediments to successful traditional business operations.[29] Such social issues as slum housing or the residential segregation of people by race must have seemed to be intractable problems fraught with so much potential for disagreement that introducing them might thwart the completion of the practicable aspects of the plan.[30]

There were also similarities in the buildings erected in each city immediately before and after the introduction of zoning and private planning. Architects and clients in one city kept abreast of interesting and useful ideas that were introduced in the other. The Wrigley Building (fig. 61) in Chicago seems to have taken some of its exterior forms from prominent examples of architecture in New York, especially the Woolworth and Municipal buildings.

Fig. 60 Cass Gilbert, Architect. George Washington Bridge, as published in the *Regional Plan of New York and Its Environs*, vol. 1 (1929).

SISTER CITIES

Fig. 61 Graham, Anderson, Probst and White, Architects. Wrigley Building, 410 North Michigan Avenue, Chicago. 1921. This photograph shows the building before its 1924 addition to the north (right).

Fig. 62 Cass Gilbert, Architect. Woolworth Building, 233 Broadway, New York. 1911-13.

From the Woolworth Building (fig. 62), Graham, Anderson, Probst and White may have taken the general design of a blocklike base with a slender tower rising in the center of the facade, and the idea of covering the steel frame with white enameled terracotta. The Municipal Building (cat. 60), designed by William Mitchell Kendall of McKim, Mead and White, may have inspired the classicistic style, the large entrance arch, and the elaborate *tempietto* on the square base that crowns the tower, even though the latter owes specific details to the Giralda Tower in Seville, Spain. When the Wrigley Building was enlarged (1924) with a new blocklike office structure to the north, the architects might have taken from the Municipal Building the idea of a screen to connect the parts. One can walk on the open plaza between the parts much as one walks through the center of the Municipal Building. The architects of the Wrigley Building also reinterpreted New York's Bankers Trust Company Building (fig. 63) in their Straus Building in Chicago (fig. 64), especially in the base-shaft-capital composition and the stepped pyramid on the roof. The more restrained London Guarantee and Accident Company Building (cat. 61) by Alfred S. Alschuler may also have borrowed from the Municipal Building its entrance arch flanked by columns, the round rooftop temple, a motif of strong verticals on the top stories (though this had been seen in Chicago, as on the Insurance Exchange of 1911-12 by D. H. Burnham and Co.), and a receding facade to accommodate an irregular but conspicuous site.[31]

The most famous of the early 20th-century connections between New York and Chicago concerned the design of the Chicago Tribune Tower in 1922 (fig. 65; cat. 62).[32] The newspaper's owner, Colonel Robert Rutherford McCormick, was as alert as William Wrigley, Jr., to the potentially handsome development of North Michigan Avenue—the "Magnificent Mile" that had been designed in connection with the Michigan Avenue Bridge (1919-20) over the Chicago River. In 1919 the newspaper company bought a large lot immediately north of railway tracks that ran at a diagonal to the riverfront, where only a low-rise soap factory interrupted the view of the site for anyone crossing the bridge. In 1920 a printing plant and newsprint storage facility designed by Jarvis Hunt was erected at the rear of the lot, leaving room along Michigan Avenue for an office tower worthy of the *Tribune*'s eminence. To draw even more attention to the newspaper, the management announced a design competition for the office building. Ten architects were invited to compete, among them Bertram G. Goodhue, Benjamin Wistar Morris, James Gamble Rogers, and John Mead Howells of New York. Two hundred fifty-nine entries were submitted, mainly by Americans, but also by architects abroad, including members of the avant- and derrière-gardes. A good many entries imitated recent eminent office buildings—for example, the beautifully drawn entry of the little-known architect Richard Yoshijiro Mine (cat. 59) was inspired by the Woolworth Building, then the tallest in the world.

John Mead Howells, who won the competition with a Gothic tower, sketched an initial design that

61

Fig. 63 Trowbridge and Livingston, Architects. Bankers Trust Company Building, Wall and Broad Streets, New York. 1912.

Fig. 64 Graham, Anderson, Probst and White, Architects. Straus Building, 310 South Michigan Avenue, Chicago. 1923.

reflected his competition project of 1908-09 for the New York Municipal Building: in its "exterior organization.... Howells expressed the verticality of the structure as well as the thinness of the masonry." Arnold Lehman, who discovered this connection, believes that Howells's preliminary Tribune sketch looks back to the New York building and forward to the final design for the Chicago building, as it is "a thinner version of the New York design with the addition of slender buttresses surrounding a very delicate lantern."[33]

But Howells, though faced with a potentially spectacular commission, did not develop the final design himself. He gave this work to Raymond Hood, who was then almost desperately unemployed and glad to be placed in charge of the competition drafting room. Howells's granddaughter has said that Howells was suffering from "intense back trouble" at the time and therefore needed an assistant,[34] but perhaps Howells had the idea that the competition was somehow weighted in his favor, for he is said to have been related to the client, Col. McCormick.[35] If so, it was a distant relationship, possibly through the Rutherford family, as Howells was the nephew of William Rutherford Mead of McKim, Mead and White who had built the Lathrop and McCormick-Patterson houses in Chicago.

For one-fifth of the $50,000 prize money, Raymond Hood worked Howells's preliminary sketch into substantially different form. One source of Hood's inspiration was the "Butter Tower" at Rouen Cathedral, which flattered the newspaper's self-image by associating its mission with spirituality. The Tribune Tower looks sturdy, as befits a building that had to project an air of substance and permanence and that commanded a site where strong winds from the lake and river would seem to threaten a weaker design. The tower's strong vertical lines and openwork crown emphasize height, as is appropriate in a tall building. The upward motion is unified, not cut up into base, shaft, and capital, and its canted corners enhance unification by easing the transition between perpendicular planes. The attention-getting lantern and buttresses on top were illuminated at night, rivaling the classical temples on the Wrigley and London Guarantee buildings across the street.

A significant connection between New York and Chicago's Tribune Tower design was made by Eliel Saarinen in his second-prize-winning design (fig. 66). Its multiple setbacks reflect the widely publicized

Fig. 65 Howells and Hood, Architects. Chicago Tribune Tower, 435 North Michigan Avenue, Chicago. 1922-24.

Fig. 66 Eliel Saarinen, Architect, with Dwight G. Wallace and Bertell Grenman, Associate Architects. Competitive Design for the Chicago Tribune Tower. 1922.

New York zoning regulations, which Saarinen may have thought would become the norm in all American cities. His nominal associates in Chicago, Bertell Grenman and Dwight G. Wallace, could have told him that Chicago was about to inaugurate its own rules regarding setbacks.

The pleasant shock of Saarinen's design reverberated to New York, and was first apparent in the American Radiator Company Building designed by Hood himself, who had earlier worked for the firm as a designer of radiator covers. Commissioned in 1923 and finished in 1924, the new building was meant to be a corporate advertisement, as the Woolworth, Singer, Wrigley, and Tribune buildings had been. In achieving this goal, Hood fashioned a setback tower much like Saarinen's, even to the placement of finials at the corners of the setbacks. The center of Hood's building, however, was emphasized by extra setback terraces rather than by Saarinen's varying fenestration and pier thickness. The most obvious difference from the Chicago project was the covering of a steel frame by black brick with gold trim (now, alas, painted a dull gold). The dark color was chosen ostensibly to unify the surface, because Hood did not like the interruptions caused by dark windows in light-colored buildings.[36] Nonetheless, as any observer can see, the windows in dark buildings create light interruptions, so surely he had another motive in mind. At the very least, it was, as Hood said, "a new plan of coloring which would make for progress." More likely, it was a way to attract notice. Hood was an ideal architect for the Jazz Age, when attention-getting stunts ranged from goldfish-swallowing to solo flights across the Atlantic. Harvey Wiley Corbett defended Hood's innovation: "If commercialism is the guiding spirit of the age, the building which advertises itself is in harmony with that spirit.... There is no reason why the term 'commercialism' should ever be considered as opposed to art."[37] A story circulated that Hood ordered red window shades that, when drawn over lighted rooms after dusk, would give the building the look of a furnace;[38] however apocryphal the story, such an act would nevertheless be in character. Hood continued to use unusual colors, in his Daily News and McGraw-Hill buildings in New York and in Ideal House (for American Radiator) in London.

Dark color made an appearance in Chicago at the Carbide and Carbon Building of 1928-29 by Hubert and Daniel Burnham. The exterior, which in both its form and its gold-trimmed dark surface recalls Hood's work, is clad in black granite up to the fourth floor and in dark green terracotta above; the entrance is covered with black marble. The terminal protuberance and the parapet decorations are picked out in gold.

In 1927 architects in Chicago and New York took different steps toward innovation, coincidentally for newspapers called the *Daily News*. Holabird and Root built "the first building in Chicago to include a public plaza as part of the development";[39] New York in these years, 1927-29, had nothing similar. The Chicago Daily News Building (fig. 67) was also the first major office in Chicago to be erected on railroad air rights. Its design includes a bland, modernized base-shaft-capital arrangement, far outclassed in glamour by the Daily News Building (fig. 68) in New York, designed by Hood with Howells and an engineering associate (later partner), J. André Fouilhoux. The 36-story New York building (1927-30) is noteworthy for its simplicity of form and surface. Smooth brick-faced piers rise straight up, and the windows are only slightly recessed, as "from the second storey to the top, there was no reason for varying a window, either in size or location."[40] At the top, Hood "tried the simple expedient of stopping without searching for or causing the owner to pay for an effect."[41] In other words, there was no parapet, spire, or pyramid there. Hood introduced rust and black brick spandrels in various geometric shapes, which are more elaborate at the bottom than on upper stories where they are hard to see. An ornamental cornice employing Chinese motifs was designed by H. V. K. Henderson for the main entrance, and a pierced sculptured screen above it depicted the

Fig. 67 Holabird and Root, Architects. Chicago Daily News Building (now Riverside Plaza), 400 West Madison Street, Chicago. 1927-29.

SISTER CITIES

Fig. 68 Raymond Hood, Architect. New York Daily News Building, 220 East 42nd Street, New York. 1927-29.

Fig. 69 Holabird and Root, Architects, with Ellerbe Architects, Associates. St. Paul City Hall — Ramsey County Courthouse, 15 Kellogg Boulevard West, St. Paul, Minnesota. 1931-32.

Fig. 70 Ralph Walker of McKenzie, Voorhees and Gmelin (later Voorhees, Gmelin and Walker), Architects. Barclay-Vesey Building (now New York Telephone Building), 140 West Street, New York. 1923-26.

Fig. 71 *Left.* Holabird and Root, Architects. 333 North Michigan Avenue, Chicago. 1927. *Right.* Alfred S. Alschuler, Architect. London Guarantee and Accident Company Building (now Stone Container Building), 360 North Michigan Avenue. 1923.

workers who created the city of skyscrapers. The aim here was to depart from traditional or familiar forms, surfaces, articulation, and ornament. In speculating on Hood's sources, John Kouwenhoven has suggested in passing that the new simplicity could have come from Fouilhoux and the interest in color from Joseph Urban.[42] Hood and Urban were good friends and, from 1928 on, collaborators on the Century of Progress fair. Perhaps the new simplicity also reflects Urban's inspiration, as he designed one of New York's only International Modern buildings, the New School for Social Research, a smooth, white prism. Fouilhoux, as far as is known, had little to do with design at any time in his American career.[43]

The New York Daily News building seems to have exerted an influence on the architects of the Chicago Daily News, for Holabird and Root designed the Ramsey County Courthouse (fig. 69) in St. Paul, Minnesota, as a tall block with setbacks between low wings.[44] It is also a simplified version of Hood's RCA Building at Rockefeller Center (for which drawings had been published in 1930), with light strips of cladding for uninterrupted vertical piers, little surface relief, and straight terminations rather than cornices. Strong verticals and colored spandrels also appeared in Holabird and Root's North Dakota State Capitol (1932-34). For metropolitan skyscrapers, the firm exercised even more restraint, retaining vestiges of the base-shaft-capital design at 333 North Michigan Avenue and the Board of Trade (1927-29), which is massed like a New York high-rise (e.g., Shelton Tower Hotel, 1923-24, by Arthur L. Harmon). Holabird and Root's Palmolive Building (1926-29; now Playboy Building) also has broad and bulky setbacks like those of the Shelton Tower, and its illuminated recessed top recalls Voorhees, Gmelin and Walker's Barclay-Vesey Telephone Building (fig. 70), opened to wide acclaim in 1926. What may be Holabird and Root's most urbanistically successful tall building, 333 North Michigan Avenue (fig. 71), is a modernized Woolworth Building. Situated at a focal point of the avenue, it commands the view with a slender tower of restrained excitement. The architects wisely controlled the elaboration and extent of the slablike, limestone-clad building behind the tower, so that the slim, tall end of the composition dominates, both on the site and in one's memory. The 333 North Michigan Avenue tower can be apprehended both up close and from a distance, unlike the Chrysler and Empire State towers in New York, which can more easily be seen from afar than from the streets below.

Another appropriate comparison to the Michigan Avenue tower may be with Howells's Panhellenic Tower (1926-28). This New York building is a sturdy shaft with canted corners, a simplified American Radiator Building that also reveals its descent from Howells and Hood's Tribune Tower and Saarinen's entry. The strong verticals and deep reveals of the Panhellenic Tower are probably based on the bell tower of St. Mark's in Venice. The skyscraper stands like a sentinel guarding a rise in the terrain, where the buildings of First Avenue changed from stockyards (on the present site of the United Nations complex) to the small shops and compact residences of the next half mile to the north.

II.
A decade of expertise in modern skyscraper development gave architects and developers in both cities the confidence to make grand plans, and three major multiple-building projects were initiated in 1928: Terminal Park, a development of enormous scope for the air rights of the Illinois Central and Michigan Central railroads on the promontory where the Chicago River meets Lake Michigan; Rockefeller Center (fig. 72); and the Century of Progress Exposition on a lakefront site south of Terminal Park.

The railroad yard promontory, a site of about 83 acres, was one too tempting to neglect, despite the problems that the venting of smoke and steam would create. The New York Central Railroad was an affiliate of lines that used the Randolph Street Station at the western end of the promontory, so that the Chicago officials could have had access to the New York Central personnel who planned the

Fig. 72 Reinhard and Hofmeister; Hood, Godley, and Fouilhoux; Corbett, Harrison and MacMurray, Associated Architects. Rockefeller Center, Fifth Avenue between 49th and 50th Streets, New York. 1929-39.

Grand Central area with its air-rights buildings. In the heady atmosphere of the late 1920s, the Illinois Central proposed a colossal building complex, the first manifestation of which was to have been the world's tallest building, 75 stories high, intended for an apparel manufacturers' mart of 4,650,000 square feet, half a million more than the Merchandise Mart now boasts. Over parking lots for Pullman cars and 1,200 automobiles were to have been two, three-story auditoriums; retail, restaurant, and convention space; 12 stories of apparel mart premises under 23 floors of offices, with 24 floors of hotel space above them; and three clubs whose members would enjoy magnificent views.[45] It was a dream of the multifunctional tower first erected in Chicago at Marina City a generation later.

Construction was supposed to have begun in 1929 and the building finished the following April, but the business arrangements must have been more complicated than the sponsors had anticipated, for by 1929 the railroads were investigating different possibilities for the site, planning the whole promontory first rather than planning around a major building. The sponsors invited proposals from three firms known for their skyscraper designs: Raymond Hood's office then called Hood, Godley, and Fouilhoux; Voorhees, Gmelin and Walker (Ralph T. Walker, chief designer); and Holabird and Root (see cat. 14). Of these, the first two firms were based in New York. The architects aligned buildings on the entire site, paying less attention to variety, open space, and public amenities than we would consider desirable if not always attainable today. They mixed high and low multiple-story buildings and allowed for air circulation, penetration of sunlight, and splendid vistas by spacing the high towers. By emphasizing symmetry, major axes, and some—if minimal—open public space along the lakefront, they preserved the sense of civic grandeur that was the lesson of the Chicago Plan.[46] Nevertheless, all three firms would probably have injured their reputation by being associated with such dense and formal development. The primary aim of the sponsors—to squeeze whatever rentable space they could from the site—is all too clear, as it is today in the buildings of Illinois Center which are going up on the same site. Although economic disaster overtook the project after the stock market crash of 1929, it is doubtful whether any such huge development could have been completed and rented even had the boom continued for a few more years. Illinois Center, originally conceived by the enlightened developer Herbert Greenwald and taken over by his successors at Metropolitan Structures, Inc., has fallen victim to other economic pressures that have vitiated some of the early ambitions for urban amenities there.[47]

Rockefeller Center, a project of apparently even greater density than Terminal Park, could become a popular and urbanistic success in part because it covers less than a quarter of the Terminal Park acreage, thereby remaining comprehensible and easy to traverse on foot.[48] Like the Chicago project, Rockefeller Center was planned from 1928 onward, also using the talents of Raymond Hood. It was realized even after the crash because John D. Rockefeller, Jr., the sponsor, had invested so much money in the lease of the property that he had to do something to force what were then 14 acres of four-story row houses and tenements to yield a greater profit, even at some time in the distant future. Rockefeller could not have commissioned undistinguished, merely expedient buildings because he had both his self-image and his investment to protect: only buildings of high quality, with such useful and pleasant features as shop-lined underground streets leading to subway connections, a midtown plaza sunk among the towers and surrounded by benches and plants, colorful, artistic decoration in easily visible and predictable places, and roof gardens, could have attracted tenants and favorable notices in the press. Rockefeller Center, a monument to enlightened self-interest, became a widely acclaimed model for corporate architecture. Designed by three firms and supervised by a developer, John R. Todd, who cared much more for profits than for modern architectural beauty, the project nevertheless showed that satisfying urban architecture might be designed by committee, although it would be hard to point to subsequent consortia that have done as well, aesthetically or financially.

The third project of 1928, the Century of Progress Exposition, was developed following a preliminary suggestion made in 1924.[49] A successful bond issue by a private exposition corporation in January 1929 provided enough money to proceed with the fair even during the Depression. The fair, a spectacular diversion from the general condition of life in 1933 and 1934, was a financial success.

The sponsors, seeking "experts" for this fair just as they had for the World's Columbian Exposition, invited out-of-town architects to suggest the best designers. The consultants were Hood and Paul Philippe Cret of Philadelphia, who, in addition to recommending their own talents, advised the sponsors to employ Harvey Wiley Corbett and Ralph T. Walker of New York, as well as Arthur Brown, Jr., of San Francisco. Eventually, Edward H. Bennett, Hubert Burnham, and John Holabird of Chicago were added to the group. The New Yorkers had appropriate experience: Corbett, in addition to being one of the planners of Rockefeller Center, had been active in civic groups that offered proposals for handling large volumes of pedestrian and vehicular traffic. Walker, the architect of complex and imaginative commercial buildings, had been one of those invited to submit plans for Terminal Park. Joseph Urban was another important contributor to the final result.

The problems of a fair were akin to those of Terminal Park or Rockefeller Center. On a site of many acres, huge numbers of people had to be channeled easily into attractive buildings where they would happily rent space, spend money, or learn to think well of a sponsor. After each architect had offered preliminary plans—which Walker said "were without too much basic understanding of the economics of exposition buildings"[50]—Hood proposed that the site be divided among the architects, with the designer of each section obliged to confer closely with his neighbors. Hood thought that the plan of the fairgrounds should not be symmetrical, as had been first proposed, but rather asymmetrical on the irregular site, so that parts could be added or reshaped without disturbing the impression of the whole area (see fig. 73).[51] The inspiration is supposed to have come to him in Amalfi, Italy,[52] where the drive along the sea might have sharpened his interest in multi-level circulation facilities and thrilling sights along a waterfront. The fair's buildings incorporated ramps that were designed to eliminate stairways and costly elevators; the architects applied lessons learned from Union Station and Grand Central Terminal. Consideration of cost eliminated the early ideas for movable sidewalks, however. Lights added to the drama of the buildings much as contemporary skyscrapers in both cities had floodlit upper stories to attract attention. The buildings incorporated innovative technology; this could be done because the fair, being built on landfill, was exempt from the Chicago building code and had a flexible code of its own. The structures, all temporary, were made of lightweight and impermanent materials. Although some of them were classicistic—like the pavilions at the 1925 Exposition des Arts Décoratifs in Paris, which offered much inspiration for this American fair—the inventive use of materials (see cat. 77) was conceptually modern. Furthermore, building ephemeral-looking structures with temporary materials was considered "honest." Corbett, when writing about the new construction, declared that buildings using such materials as gypsum board and aluminum "certainly...could not simulate masonry" and that carved "ornament, which had its origin in masonry, could not appropriately be used."[53] The use of gypsum-board cladding for lightweight frames meant that the buildings had to be painted,

SISTER CITIES

Fig. 73 Edward H. Bennett, Daniel H. Burnham, Jr., Arthur Brown, Harvey Corbett, Paul Cret, John Holabird, Raymond Hood, and Ralph Walker, Architects. Aerial view of the Century of Progress Exposition, Chicago. 1933 (now demolished).

as the gypsum component would have been all but dissolved by wind and rain. The aluminum color that was tried at first yielded to rainbow hues chosen by William Muschenheim under Urban's supervision.[54] Color, which, as we have seen above, had recently enhanced the Carbide and Carbon Building, as well as buildings in New York by Ely Jacques Kahn, Raymond Hood, and others, became one of the most memorable features of the fair. Corbett emphasized the novelty of the buildings, the asymmetry of planning, and the overall composition, recanting his own earlier teaching that "symmetry and balance were architectural essentials," now preferring whatever plans met "such considerations as movement and circulation."[55] Kahn was pleased that the architects had "unanimously attempted to study their buildings in masses, avoiding the usual collection of mongrel sculpture." Other aspects of the fair drew his praise: "There is practically no ornament; the surfaces are broken into various planes often to permit light sources to develop interesting forms.... There is little of sham, either in construction or architectural design." He found the "color statement...the most vital contribution to a new architecture."[56]

From a later perspective, we see that the 1933 fair introduced many people to unfamiliar architectural forms, novel effects of light and color, and new materials. It helped to accustom Americans to new aspects of technology and to modern prefabrication. The cable-hung, domed Travel and Transport Building was the first suspended enclosed structure in the country. George Fred Keck's polygonal House of Tomorrow (fig. 74) was constructed of many prefabricated parts, some of them plastic, and it included central air conditioning and an all-electric kitchen. The fair also marked the first important appearance of the brothers-in-law Louis Skidmore and Nathaniel Owings, respectively Chief of Design and Supervisor of Development, who together at Hood's direction produced the sketch of the first of the asymmetrical fairground plans.

The New York World's Fair of 1939-40 was also supposed to make a profit although there was a deficit in the end; like the Century of Progress, it was located on land that was filled or improved to become a public park[57] although the original plans for what is now New York's Flushing Meadow Park have yet to be completed. As a nominally private enterprise, the fair corporation did not receive direct government subsidy, but city, state, and federal governments paid for pavilions, access roads and bridges, grading, utility planning, and planting, without which the fair could not have taken place.

Fig. 74 George Fred Keck, Architect. The House of Tomorrow, Century of Progress Exposition, Chicago. 1933 (now demolished).

In plan and in architectural design, New York's fair was more classicistic and symmetrical than Chicago's. Despite the presence of dramatic lighting, some colored pavilions, and a "Town of Tomorrow" (fig. 75) with homes comparable to models shown in Chicago, the 1939 fair was a more formal and staid place; even the color palette was virtually limited to primary colors and white. The asymmetrical plan of 1933 hardened into the formal plan of 1939, just as Chicago's colorful, irregular, and consciously ephemeral rainbow of buildings froze into the icicle of the Trylon and Perisphere (fig. 28), the main architectural features in New York. They were a 750-foot-high tapering shaft and a globe 200 feet in diameter, designed by Wallace Harrison and J. André Fouilhoux, who were then putting up the last buildings at Rockefeller Center. The designers were more conservative, on the whole, and went back to basics: the plan reflected the classical tradition, and theme buildings utilized elemental geometric forms. Both the homage to tradition and the effect of visual stability were ironic, in that war broke out on September 1, 1939, before the fair was over. But even before this event it was clear that the stability of the plan and the design of many of the pavilions conflicted with the changes in modern living that were announced by the displays. While the exhibitions showed modern homes using electricity, lightweight metals, and new synthetic fabrics, and while above all, new automobiles were prominent attractions, fake old world villages and the authority of old master paintings maintained an illusion that domestic change and the new chaos abroad could be kept at bay. The plan and its imposing buildings accurately revealed important alterations that had already occurred. The huge scale and imposing formality mirrored the size of the government agencies that were directing much of American life in the 1930s under the expansive policies of the Roosevelt administration. They reflected, too, the growing managerial, rather than entrepreneurial, spirit in corporations and government agencies. Some of the ponderous national pavilions even seemed to be images of the dictatorships in the world. Folke Tyko Kihlstedt, in an illuminating comparison of the 1933 and 1939 fairs, has observed that in the technological theme of the 1939 fair one could see that the world of the future was one that demanded a good manager.[58] An emphasis on inventive science in 1933 had yielded to the theme of "demonstrating not mere mechani-

SISTER CITIES

cal progress...but the ways in which new machines and merchandise could be used to improve economic conditions"—to quote the worlds of a government-sponsored guide book.[59]

III.
Since the Second World War, the business districts in Chicago and New York have drawn closer architecturally, as corporations have generated comparable buildings. There are many feeble versions of the Lever and Seagram headquarters, many blank-walled hulks, and too many windows that cannot open. It is hard to decide whether the clash of Water Tower Place with the neighboring Hancock Center in Chicago is worse than the pile-up of new skyscrapers in New York on Madison Avenue around 56th Street. A generation of more flamboyant buildings has supplanted the simpler slabs of the years just after the war. Chicago's One Magnificent Mile and the Madison-Wells project, both by Skidmore, Owings and Merrill (see fig. 77), bid for popular attention just as New York's Citicorp Center by Hugh Stubbins did, for each has a sloping tower top. One Magnificent Mile even has a sloping low building beside the tower as Citicorp does—an entrance in Chicago, a church in New York.

The spirit or at least the forms of the roaring twenties have returned, bringing designs which enliven the skyline. The most famous is the A T & T Building (fig. 76) in New York, designed by Philip Johnson with John Burgee, with Harry Simmons as associate. The press release distributed by A T & T alerts us to the architects' intentions that

> the structure should "recall" the buildings that gave New York its architectural greatness—such structures as the famous Century Club, Morgan Library, and Columbia University buildings of the 1890s and the American Radiator, Daily News, and Rockefeller Center buildings of the 1920s.... The design would represent greater values than a "glass box" could contain. We wanted something that would make people say, "That must be the AT&T Building."[60]

In Chicago, architect Stanley Tigerman even invited his contemporaries to submit "late entries" (see cat. 64) to the Chicago Tribune competition of 1922![61] Helmut Jahn of Murphy/Jahn has just completed the Board of Trade Addition and One South Wacker Drive (fig. 77), where the upper parts of the surface are divided into long strips, using black and transparent glass as if he were referring to striped building designs of the interwar years. In New York, the surfaces of the Singer Building (cat. 56) and the City Bank Farmers' Trust Company Building at 20

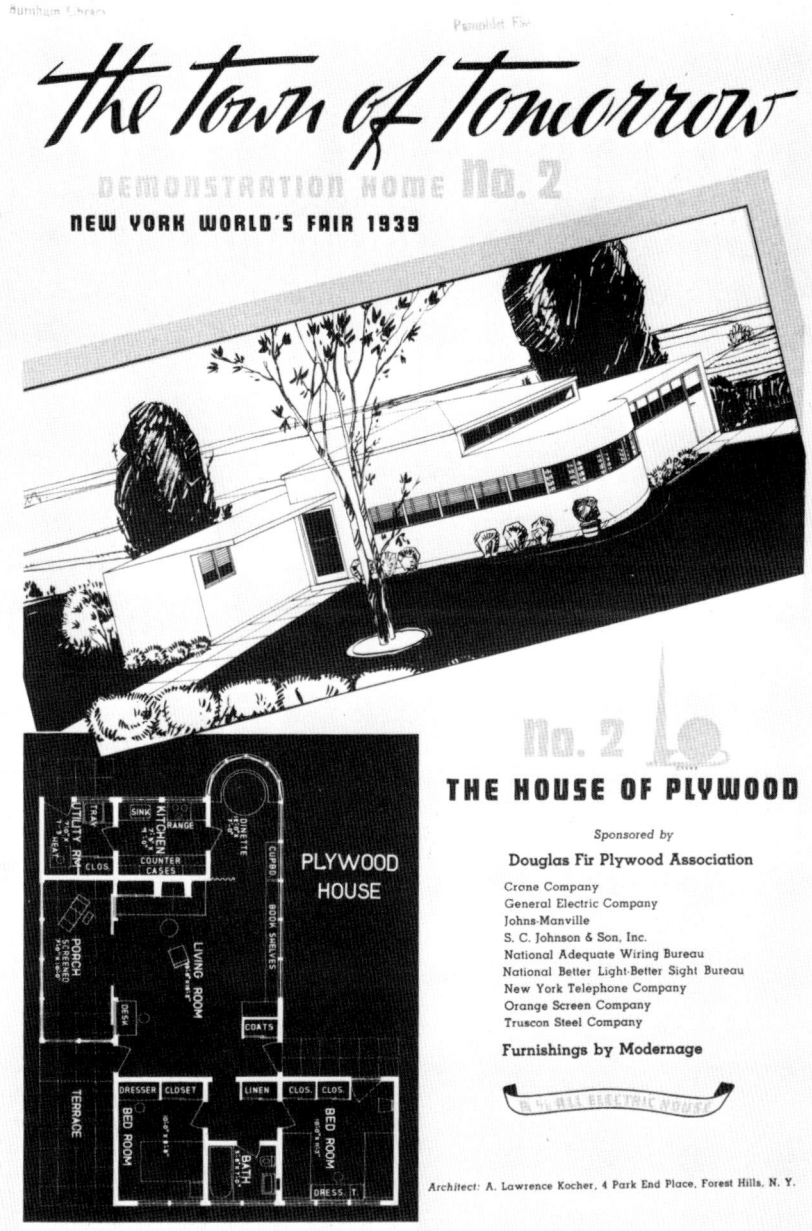

Fig. 75 A. Lawrence Kocher, Architect. The House of Plywood in the Town of Tomorrow, World's Fair, New York. 1939 (now demolished).

71

Fig. 76 Aerial photograph, taken in 1983, of midtown Manhattan, showing at center the A T & T Building.

Fig. 77 Aerial photograph, taken in 1983, of South Wacker Drive, Chicago, showing 333 West Wacker Drive, Madison-Wells, and 1 South Wacker Drive Buildings.

Exchange Place/22 William Street (Cross and Cross, 1930-31) had long ago been cut up by using the dark and light facing materials of their times.

Several recent designs revive the streamlined modernism of the Depression years—as is, perhaps, appropriate to our present decade of economic uncertainty. The Operations Center for Irving Trust Company of New York (fig. 78) by Skidmore, Owings and Merrill has ribbon windows and setbacks like something by Kahn and Jacobs from the years before the Second World War. Helmut Jahn, who designed the Xerox Centre (fig. 79) in Chicago, has planned to replace the North Western Railroad Station with a skyscraper that is a mass of cascading glass, a bright Hollywoodish form of one of Hugh Ferriss's looming visions, with some references to the lobby of the Chicago Board of Trade Building (by Holabird and Root, 1929) and with a doorway inspired by Louis Sullivan's portal for the Transportation Building at the World's Columbian Exposition.[62] In New York, Davis, Brody and Associates has designed a 35-story apartment house in a comparable style for West 68th Street and Broadway that crosses the massing of the RCA Building with the horizontal bands of the McGraw-Hill Building, or with the horizontal bands and almost-curving corners of the Starrett-Lehigh Building. The Gruzen Partnership has designed another apartment house (cat. 38), on Broadway at 87th Street, in a style used around 1930 by the office of Irwin S. Chanin and by Emery Roth for the Century and San Remo apartments (cat. 37), respectively—complete with twin towers, a mixture of limestone and brick facing, and windows that wrap around the corners of the towers. Most spectacular of all are Cesar Pelli's designs for Battery Park City (fig. 80), which recalls Rockefeller Center

Fig. 78 Raul DeArmas and Gordon Wildermuth of Skidmore, Owings and Merrill, Architects. Preliminary Model of Irving Trust Company Building, 101 Barclay Street, New York. 1980-83.

Fig. 79 Helmut Jahn of C. F. Murphy and Associates, Architects. Xerox Centre, 55 West Monroe Street, Chicago. 1975-80.

Fig. 80 Cesar Pelli and Associates, Architects. World Financial Center or Proposed Battery Park Towers, New York. 1983. Photomontage by Richard Baehr.

in coordination and ambition. It even has low, nine-story buildings to frame the entrance to the project, like Rockefeller Center's seven-story ones. Pelli himself has said, "The form of the buildings derives from a synthesis of the prismatic form of the postwar high-rise building with the New York City skyscraper of the '20s and '30s.... Stepped forms cause the buildings to ascend visually."[63] The last statement, if true, is an accidental consequence of the 1916 zoning rules.

Most affirmatively, citizens of both Chicago and New York have improved open public spaces, enjoyed the stimulus to skylines that were becoming clumsy and flat on top, experimented with new zoning rules, and saved many designated landmarks from demolition. New York adopted Chicago's idea of buildings for mixed office, shop, and apartment use.[64] Chicago's Marina, Hancock, and Sears towers inspired the Galleria, Olympic, Trump, and other buildings executed since about 1970 in midtown Manhattan.

IV.
Despite many similarities, New York and Chicago do not look alike. Obviously, one city grew on an island between rivers near an ocean bay, with irregular terrain and solid bedrock under only certain parts of it—notably lower Manhattan and midtown, where the skyscrapers are concentrated. The other city spread itself out on low-lying land along one side of an enormous lake. Expansion in New York required spectacular feats of engineering like bridges and subways. The 17th-century growth of lower Manhattan affected the subsequent city profoundly: upon it now rests a tightly packed cluster of tall buildings on narrow streets. In the next century and a half—before Chicago was even founded—open squares of English Georgian inspiration were introduced. These early developments are absent from the much younger Chicago. The grid of 1807-11 that was imposed on New York by unimaginative commissioners was unlike Chicago's grid of mid-century, for Manhattan's was irregular and was interrupted at unpredictable intervals by Broadway, which created triangular blocks and open spaces that are found in Chicago only when an old road intersected with the grid outside the city center. The two cities' building rules created other differences, including the mandated alleys between buildings in Chicago, which contrast with the solid street fronts of New York. As stated earlier, the cities also have different height limits and setback regulations. New York's streets offer more textural density, partly due to the older age and the varied character of many surviving buildings. Scale, style, materials, spacing, height—all seem to vary in the central and lower Manhattan business districts more than they do in Chicago. Manhattan's solid street lines contribute to this impression, as does the greater number of buildings over three stories in height.

Chicago replaces New York's rich variety with invigorating openness. The wide grids of the Loop and the rest of the city are regular and predictable. There is space between many buildings. The high-rises are relatively new, and both the buildings and the streets seem cleaner. There is a brilliant contrast of tall, man-made monuments on Michigan Avenue with the natural expanse of the great lake, and there are light and openness at the north end of North Michigan Avenue where air and water conclude the promenade. The welcome expanse of the open river on two more sides of the commercial heart of Chicago is especially distinctive. Manhattan's buildings generally diminish in height east of Third and west of Eighth Avenue, creating a pyramid with its apex on the island's central spine and the base along the water, a configuration different from Chicago's rectangle between the river and the lake. The relief offered by Central Park, a complex contrivance enclosed in stone walls that follow the grid, is quite different from that of the wide-open parkland along Lake Michigan. But the overall effect of both cities is exhilarating, and they are richer for their exchange of ideas and influences. They are, in many ways, clearly siblings who have influenced each other, and we are the richer because they are not identical twins.

Notes

I am grateful to Diana L. Murphy for her careful work in providing articles used in the preparation of this essay, and to John Zukowsky for making available recent materials on Chicago that are not yet in New York libraries.

1. For these residential projects, see Arthur Drexler, *The Drawings of Frank Lloyd Wright* (New York, 1962), drawings nos. 120-23. For the exhibition house, see "Frank Lloyd Wright Builds in the Middle of Manhattan," *House and Home* 4 (Nov. 1953), pp. 118-21, and *The Usonian House. Souvenir of the Exhibition: Sixty Years of Living Architecture. The Work of Frank Lloyd Wright* (New York: Guggenheim Museum, 1953).

2. Carl W. Condit, *Chicago, 1910-29: Building, Planning, and Urban Technology* (Chicago, 1973), p. 46.

3. See also City Club of Chicago, *The Railway Terminal Problem of Chicago* (Chicago, 1913).

4. Condit (note 2), pp. 253-60; Peter B. Wight, "The Chicago and Northwestern Rail Road Company's Passenger Terminal Building at Chicago," *Building Progress* 1 (July 1911), p. 197.

5. For the most recent and authoritative account of these two complexes, see Carl W. Condit, *The Port of New York*, vol. 1, *A History of Rail Terminal Systems from the Beginning to Pennsylvania Station* (Chicago and London, 1980), pp. 181-258, and vol. 2, *A History of the Rail and Terminal Systems from the Grand Central Electrification to the Present* (Chicago and London, 1981), pp. 1-100. See also David Marshall, *Grand Central* (New York, 1946).

6. Condit (note 2), p. 55 n. 12.

7. Peter B. Wight, "The Life and Works of Rafael Guastavino," *Brickbuilder* 10 (April, May, Sept., Oct. 1901), pp. 78-81, 100-02, 184-88, 211-14; George Collins, "The Transfer of Thin Masonry Vaulting from Spain to America," *Journal of the Society of Architectural Historians* 27 (Oct. 1968), pp. 176-201.

8. Condit (note 2), pp. 264-84.

9. Ibid., pp. 141-42.

10. "The Hudson and Manhattan Terminal Buildings, Clinton and Russell, Architects," *Architects' and Builders' Magazine* 9 (1907-08), pp. 456-70. No engineer is named here. For excellent pictures, see Moses King, *King's Views of New York, 1896-1915, and Brooklyn 1905*, ed. A. Santaniello (New York, 1980), p. 2.

11. *New York Times*, June 26, 1930, p. 42; Nov. 29, 1931, sec. 11-12, p. 1. No engineer is named here. The building does not seem to have been published in periodicals indexed in the *Engineering Index*.

12. Frank P. Sengstock, "The Largest Building in the World," *Western Architext* 39 (Dec. 1930), pp. 205-07.

13. Robert Moses, *Public Works: A Dangerous Trade* (New York, 1970), p. 184; Werner Hegemann, *City Planning and Housing*, vol. 3, *A Graphic Review of Civic Art*, ed. William W. Forster and Robert C. Weinberg (New York, 1938), p. 63, fig. 446.

14. The Loop elevated railway was built in the years 1893 to 1896.

15. Moses (note 13), p. 185.

16. Sarah Bradford Landau, "The Tall Office Building Artistically Reconsidered: Arcaded Buildings of the New York School, c. 1870-1890," in *In Search of Modern Architecture: A Tribute to Henry-Russell Hitchcock*, ed. Helen Searing (New York, 1982), pp. 136-64.

17. Masami Takayama, "'Good Buildings, Cheap': Interview with John A. Holabird," in *Process Architecture #35: The Chicago School of Architecture* (Tokyo, 1982), pp. 22-23.

18. Ibid.

19. *Report of the Heights of Buildings Commission to the Committee on the Height, Size, and Arrangement of Buildings of the Board of Estimate and Apportionment of the City of New York*, Dec. 23, 1913, pp. 18-19.

20. "Subway System and Land Values," *New York Times*, July 27, 1912, sec. 8, p. 2; for other aspects of congestion and land value, see "Excessive Height Reduces Rentals in Neighborhood," *New York Times*, Nov. 2, 1913, sec. 8, p. 1. For an economic analysis after the boom years, see William Clark, *The Skyscraper* (New York, 1930).

21. Seymour Toll, *Zoned America* (New York, 1969, p. 71; *Report* (note 19), p. 17.

22. *Report* (note 19), p. 15. Economic analysis in this report and in G. C. Nimmons, "The Passing of the skyscraper," *Journal of the American Insitute of Architects* 10 (Nov. 1922), failed to persuade builders to reduce office tower heights. High-speed elevators, air conditioning, and fluorescent lighting, which open more of the interior volume to rentable space, have altered the basis for estimating the cost-benefit ration of high-rise buildings; see Reyner Banham, *The Architecture of the Well-Tempered Environment* (Chicago and London, 1969), pp. 171-283. An incalculable benefit has always been the value of the publicity given by a beautiful, very tall, or otherwise conspicous building.

23. For early zoning, see U.S. Department of Commerce, *Zoning: A Selected Bibliography*, ed. T. Kimball, rev. ed. (Washington, D.C., 1922, mimeographed.)

24. W. H. Wilson, "Moles and Skylarks," in *Coming of Age: Urban America 1915-1945* (New York, 1974), reprinted in *Introduction to Planning History in the United States*, ed. Donald A. Krueckeberg (New Brunswick, 1983), p. 90.

25. Condit (note 2), p. 168 n. 15.

26. These figures come from Walter H. Blucher, "Zoning and Quitting," in *Proceedings of the First Annual Indiana State-Wide Planning Conference* (n.p., 1938), p. 41.

27. Constance Perin, *Everything in its Place: Social Order and Land Use in America* (Princeton, 1977), pp. 32-80, 129-62.

28. Committee on the Regional Plan of New York and Its Environs, *Regional Survey of New York and Its Environs*, 8 vols. (New York, 1927-31.)

29. Wilson (note 24), pp. 99-101, has additional brief remarks on this matter, which are milder than those of Lewis Mumford, "The Plan of New York," *New Republic* 71 (June 15, 1932), pp. 121-26, and "The Plan of New York, II" *New Republic* 71 (June 22, 1932), pp. 146-54. Mumford was Secretary of the Regional Planning Association of America, not to be confused with the Regional Plan Association, Inc., which was founded later to work for the adoption of the Russell Sage-sponsored Regional Plan.

30. Some cities tried to zone separate black and white housing areas, but this was ruled unconstitutional; cf. Edward Bassett, *Zoning* (New York, 1940), p. 49.

31. See John Zukowsky, *Architecture in Context: 360 North Michigan Avenue* (Chicago, 1981), with further bibliography.

32. *The Chicago Tribune International Competition* (Chicago, 1923); see Manfredo Tafuri, "The Disenchanted Mountain: The Skyscraper and the City," in Giorgio Ciucci et al., *The American City from the Civil War to the New Deal* (New Cambridge, Mass., 1979), pp. 389-421; and Robert A. M. Stern and Thomas Catalano, *Raymond Hood* (New York, 1982), pp. 102-03, for bibliographical references for all of Hood's works.

33. Arnold Lehman, "The New York Skyscraper: A History of its Development, 1870-1939" (Ph.D. diss., Yale University, 1974), p. 228 n. 4.

34. Quoted in Lehman (note 33), p. 228 n. 4.

36. I gathered this information from the historian Cynthia Field and architect Wallace K. Harrison, although neither knew what the precise relationship was. I have been unable to trace it in genealogies of the McCormick, Mead, and Rutherford families.

37. "The regular spacing of these black holes," said Hood, "makes a building look like waffles or doormats hung up to dry." *New York Times*, Jan. 20, 1924.

37. Harvey Wiley Corbett, "The American Radiator Building, New York City," *Architectural Record* 55 (May 1924), p. 474. In 1930 the architect John Harbeson wrote that buildings such as the Woolworth and Singer were designed like posters or advertisements to attract attention. He found this a recent development; see "Design in Modern Architecture," *Pencil Points* 11 (Jan. 1930), p. 9.

38. Walter Kilham, Jr., who worked for Hood at the end of the decade, observed that "for a company selling furnaces, a building that glowed in the dark...was not such a wild idea." *Raymond Hood* (New York, 1973), p. 70.

39. Condit (note 2), p. 121.

40. Raymond M. Hood, "The News Building," *Architectural Forum* 53 (Nov. 1930), p. 531.

41. Ibid.

42. John Kouwenhoven, *Made in America* (Garden City, 1948), p. 252.

43. Interview with Wallace K. Harrison. The documents concerning the planning of Rockefeller Center support Mr. Harrison's statement.

44. Robert Bruegmann, "Holabird & Roche and Holabird & Root: The First Two Generations," *Chicago History* 9 (Fall 1980), pp. 130-65, with annotated bibliography.

45. "Huge Mart to Top our Tracks," *Illinois Central Magazine* 17 (July 1928), pp. 5-7.

46. Holabird and Root's drawings have been donated to The Art Institute of Chicago; Ralph Walker's, which were part of his firm's project (no. 764), were in the custody of his successor firm, Haines Lundberg Waehler of New York. Walker published the joint drawings for it in his autobiography, *Ralph Walker, Architect* (New York, 1957), pp. 43-47, and claimed that the drawings were made in his office. These drawings have been published by Stern and Catalano (note 32) as Hood's. The Avery Library, Columbia University, has Fouilhoux's portfolio of photographs of the joint project (Palmer Shannon Cameragraphs).

47. For an enlightening conversation, an examination of plans, and a tour of the site, I am indebted to Irving Cherry, former Senior Vice-President of Metropolitan Structures, Inc. For more recent developments, see M. W. Newman, "The Illinois Center Build-up," *Inland Architect* 17 (Dec. 1973), pp. 12-16; for the first two buildings (i.e., Illinois Center #1 by Mies van der Rohe, and Illinois Center #2 by the Office of Mies van der Rohe, Joseph Fujikawa, Job Captain, with structural engineers Farkas and Barron and mechanical engineers Cosentini Associates), see "Chicago Frame-Up," *Architectural Forum* 140 (Jan.-Feb. 1974), pp. 74-79.

48. For recent accounts of the Center, see Carol Herselle Krinsky, *Rockefeller Center* (New York, 1978); Alan Balfour, *Rockefeller Center: Architecture as Theater* (New York, 1978); Ciucci et al. (note 32), pp. 461-83.

49. I am grateful to John Zukowsky for putitng at my disposal some of the Burnham Library's abundant holdings on this fair. A wide range of publications on the fair may be found in the published catalogues of the Burnham Library, Avery Library, and the New York Public Library.

50. Walker (note 46), p. 85.

51. Ibid.

52. Kilham (note 38), p. 108. See also Louis Skidmore, "Planning and Planners," *Architectural Forum* 59 (July 1933), p. 32.

53. Harvey Wiley Corbett, "The Significance of the Exposition," *Architectural Forum* 59 (July 1933), p. 1.

54. For information about the gypsum board and the responsibility of color selection, I am indebted to the late Otto J. Teegen, who was sent by Urban to supervise the execution of the color and obtained special pigments for it.

55. Corbett (note 53), p. 1.

56. Ely Jacques Kahn, "Close-Up Comments on the Fair," *Architectural Forum* 59 (July 1933), pp. 23-24. For a critical look at the fair, see Henry-Russell Hitchcock, Jr., "Notes on architecture, Chicago, 1933," *Hound and Horn* 7 (Oct.-Dec. 1933), pp. 133-36.

57. Moses (note 13), p. 539. For the fair itself, see *Official Souvenir Book: New York World's Fair, 1939* (New York, 1939) and *Official Guide Book: The World's Fair of 1940 in New York* (New York, 1940). The planning reports may conveniently be followed by reference to the *New York Times Index*, especially the years 1938 and 1939.

58. Folke Tyko Kihlstedt, "American Modernism and the Architecture of the Expositions of Chicago (1933) and New York (1939)" (Paper delivered at the Annual Meeting of the Society of Architectural Historians, Philadelphia, 1976).

59. The emphasis on science, albeit partly for the sake of lively public relations, was mady by Louis Skidmore, "Science Dictates the Building Mode for 1933," *T-Square Club Journal* 1 (June 1931), pp. 20-21. The new theme was expressed in Lou Gody, ed., *New York City Guide: The Federal Writers' Project* (New York, 1939), p. 629.

60. A T & T, "Fact Sheet," Feb. 17, 1983. I thank A T & T for providing me with this material.

61. Stanley Tigerman, ed., *Chicago Tribune Tower and Late Entries* (New York, 1980).

62. John Zukowsky, "Chicago's Architectural Exhibits: The Historical Background," in *Beyond the International Style: New Chicago Architecture*, ed. Maurizio Casari and Vincenzo Pavan (Verona, 1981), p. 79. See also *Chicago Architects Design: A Century of Architectural Drawings from The Art Institute of Chicago* (Chicago, 1982), p. 135.

63. "Cesar Pelli's Winning Design for Commercial Core of Battery Park City," *Architectural Record* 169 (July 1981), p. 41.

64. Blaine A. Brownell and Clifford C. Johnson, "Cities within a City: The Origins of Three Multi-Use Buildings in Chicago," *Architectural Forum* 140 (Jan.-Feb. 1974), pp. 38-43.

Commentaries on Chicago and New York

In the spirit of pluralism, the Department of Architecture at The Art Institute of Chicago asked architects, critics, historians, and preservationists to contribute a statement about architectural interactions between Chicago and New York — i.e., what they felt the essence of this interaction has been in the past and where it might lead in the next generation. The following commentaries were received from those who were kind enough to take the time to think about this question.

Laurence Booth
Architect, Chicago

New York is always grown up...assured.
Chicago is always adolescent...vigorous.
New York verifies, establishes, knows.
Chicago hunts, tries, hopes.
New York is the boundary, the front door.
Chicago is the middle surrounded by America.
New York has given Chicago:
   McKim and the classical ideal...a standard.
   The Standard Oil Building...poised and proper.
Chicago has given New York:
   The Bayard Building...Sullivan's American vision.
   The Flatiron Building...Vitruvius Americana.
   The Seagram Building...a new standard.
   The Guggenheim...something fresh.

Every house has a front room for grown-ups to sit and a back room where kids wrestle and where the pots are stirred. America needs these two rooms ... the New York parlor and the Chicago kitchen ... and we will always need to go from one room into the other.

Stuart Cohen
Architect, Chicago

Mies's dictum, "Build, don't talk," has been taken to characterize the difference between the architectural activities of Chicago and New York. Thus, we would expect that Chicago would look to New York as a source of theory (what to build) and of philosophy (why to build) and that New York would look to Chicago as a source of practice (how to build). This has not always been the case. Louis Sullivan and Frank Lloyd Wright were important theoreticians just as prominent New York architects from Stanford White to Philip Johnson have been important builders. At the 1893 World's Columbian Exposition, New York and Chicago's most important architectural interaction, it was New Yorker Charles F. McKim who proposed that the fair buildings be neoclassical and it was Chicagoan Daniel H. Burnham who foresaw the theoretical importance of this decision for American city planning.

While we could ascribe differences between Chicago and New York to location — civilization versus frontier — as an explanation of why one city might excel in art and another in technology, perhaps the characterization of New York as theoretical and Chicago as practical is not the only one with which to approach the question of their architectural interaction. Since New York is a city seemingly dedicated to the idea of change while Chicago is a city of cultural conservatism, I would propose that their interaction be considered in these terms: that Chicago has received from New York the forms of an architecture representative of progress and change (European modernism) and that Chicago has given New York, via the skyscrapers of the first and second "Chicago Schools of Architecture" (including Mies's American work), an architecture expressive of stability and power. John Wellborn Root believed this architecture could "convey in some large elemental sense an idea of the great, stable, conserving forces of modern civilization."

Carl W. Condit
Professor Emeritus
Northwestern University

There are profound and pervasive differences between New York and Chicago with respect to their history, their intrinsic character, and their national role, distinctions that are clearly reflected in the architectural expression of the two cities. Foremost among them is simple chronological age: New York has existed as a city more than 350 years, two centuries beyond Chicago's urban life. As a consequence, New York has recapitulated very nearly the entire post-Renaissance development of the buildings arts. As the rapidly expanding port city approached the status of a world metropolis at the end of the 19th century, it was well on the way to creating the largest body of great commercial architecture in the world. By the turn of the century its achievements in commercial and public building reached a pre-eminence so far in the front rank that European architects were looking to the city for models, and European governments began to send official deputations to study the city's chief architectural works.

In its size, functional complexity, technical audacity, diversity, and richness of form, the New York skyscraper by the time of the First World War had eclipsed anything comparable to it. The architectural grandeur and technological primacy of the city's electrified railroad stations—the largest ever constructed — led to their recognition as the foremost works of their kind and possibly America's supreme achievements in the building arts. The zoning ordinance of 1916 stood among the most forward-looking and most far-reaching acts of its kind, simultaneously establishing control over the reckless growth of the skyscraper and powerfully stimulating architectural inventiveness in the formal treatment of high buildings.

New York unquestionably created the first skyscraper in the Equitable Life Assurance Building (1868-71) and in little more than forty years carried it to a spectacular culmination in the Woolworth Building (1911-13). New York architects created the first Art Deco skyscraper in the Barclay-Vesey Telephone Building (1923-26), combining in it the expression of structure, function, and internal space with that of human needs and responses on both the physical and spiritual level. In short, the architects solved the problem of giving warmth, richness, and humanity as well as visual power to the modern office block. Needless to say, the solution was subsequently forgotten. The architects and planners of Rockefeller Center produced what Vincent Scully called the "finest spatial grouping of skyscrapers in America." The great architectural achievements of commercial Chicago were largely concentrated in two decades, the 1890s and the 1920s. In New York they were spread lavishly over 70 years. As for the quality of this architecture, taken in its totality, I think it is impossible to place one city before the other. Each reveals in its building art its own history, setting, and modes of community life.

Paul Gapp
Chicago Tribune Architecture Critic

The 20th century's most influential architect was Ludwig Mies van der Rohe, who taught and practiced in Chicago for 30 years and whose methods dominated architecture in virtually every major American city. Those methods were, in a superficial sense, easily learned, and thus employed by hack architects as well as distinguished designers. They coincided perfectly with changes in technology and commercial space needs. They were embraced by the nation's largest architecture firm, the Chicago-founded Skidmore, Owings and Merrill. So powerful was Mies's influence that other architectural interactions or influences between Chicago and New York are by comparison relatively minor.

The Chicago School (to which Mies sounded a thunderous reprise) and its eminent practitioners were mostly ignored in New York. So was Frank Lloyd Wright. Too much has been made, probably, of Eliel Saarinen's second-place entry in the Chicago Tribune competition and other codified occurrences. Looking at matters the other way around, New York's skill at Art Deco and kindred styles was hardly lost on Chicago, although relatively few large-scale examples of Art Deco exist in Chicago. New York may be said to have invented zoning after a Chicago architect perpetrated Manhattan's immensely bulky Equitable Building in 1915, but any obliquely salutary effect zoning had on the massing of skyscrapers was transitory. In any event, zoning has since inspired more design mischief than progress in both cities.

Of the future, who can say? Having broken out of their Miesian straitjackets later than New York designers, Chicago architects are now the equals of their Eastern brethren in the creation of New Mainstream architecture—which is to say the notching, twisting, and setbacking of high-rise envelopes into shapes reminiscent of the 1930s. This leaves Postmodernism, of which Chicago's Helmut Jahn is among the most radical and certainly the nation's most prolific adherent. It also leaves salon and art journal architecture (the kind that never gets built), at which New Yorkers have always excelled. In the new world of pluralism, it will be harder to tell who is interacting with whom. That will make life harder for future art historians seeking facile connections, but it may also make it clearer that all significant American architecture is not made only in New York and Chicago.

Bruce J. Graham
Architect, Chicago

Chicago architecture has naturally been affected, both directly and indirectly, by architects from around the world, and similar influences have shaped New York. But the primary influences of Chicago on New York can probably be traced to technical events rather than architectural influences. Skyscrapers and elevators traveled from west to east, but they traveled lightly since the vocabulary essentially remained in Chicago until it leapfrogged to Europe, primarily London, Liverpool, and Paris. In terms of architectural vocabulary, William Le Baron Jenney, Louis Sullivan, or Holabird and Root had little, if any, influence on the classical revivalists with whom they coexisted. There is, however, a powerful influence on Chicago architects from the East, not limited to New York, which has affected deeply the character of buildings in this city. Frank Furness in Philadelphia had a direct link to Sullivan and remained an influence throughout his life. H. H. Richardson influenced the Prairie houses by local example as well as by the power of his ideas. Raymond Hood brought to Chicago his vision of buildings where structure disappeared and sculpture predominated.

Daniel H. Burnham, during and after the World's Fair, imparted the latest concepts best expressed by Stanford White, concepts which were not comfortable in a city searching for an industrial and agricultural expression, but he did succeed in creating a vision of open space through the imagery of parks and boulevards which were foreign to the Midwestern city, but which found an immediate response and have affected the vision of Chicago architects since that time. He was able to integrate these concepts within the ever-present grid of the farmlands. This gives Chicago its form and its spirit.

There is a basic difference between New York City and Chicago. Our city is barely one hundred years old, located in a land with no boundaries and surrounded, if you please, by a lake without character and a prairie without limit. Buildings, therefore, end up with the spatial character of containing bits of larger lonely space. It matters little whether it is a silo on the horizon or the Hancock Building along the lakefront: they immediately take on a character that probably is only matched by the steppes of Russia or the Arab towers in the Sahara.

New York, on the other hand, has already undergone the overbuilding of Rome, one civilization upon another, establishing meaningful relationships to previous civilizations. In some cases, like Rome, you end up with barbarians camping on the residue of the past. The edges and limits are well defined and have a direct influence on the character of its citizens.

There is no past to Chicago, so the transfers from New York to Chicago have by and large been painterly and sculptural, not architectural or spatial. This does not mean that there is not today, like in the past, a communication of ideas, as to detail which influences us both. Perhaps this sort of language is international architecture, and it is best tested in America before we export it to the rest of the world. The single most powerful external influence in the last twenty years comes, not from New York, but from Germany. Mies van der Rohe, however, influenced all architects by the discovery of a contemporary vocabulary which is now being elaborated upon by all architects, but whose imprint was most adaptable to the industrial, rather than to the commercial city.

Richard Haas
Architectural Artist, New York

The general notion is that many if not most ideas about architecture, and what a city should be, came from Europe and filtered from the East westward, most often from New York. When ideas reached Chicago, however, something else seemed to happen. It may have been due, at least in part, to the geography: large flat expanses and an unrelenting grid were antithetical to cities superimposed over Dutch or English Georgian townscapes. Besides this there was the frontyard effect of Lake Michigan, as opposed to the bay, estuary, and ocean effects of New York. These geographic differences created the strong north-south axis of Manhattan and very separate communities in other boroughs, as opposed to the overall gridiron effect of Chicago away from the lake. The broad block horizontality of Chicago helped to shape its architecture, as the 20-, 40-, and 50-foot Dutch lots shaped New York.

New York, I think, was also more about a sense of style than innovation. Style adapted and then reshaped on a scale never conceived before. The Woolworth and Municipal buildings and the early Wall Street structures exemplify this. Chicago was a place of both daring innovation and stylistic development, but there the innovation seemed to dominate. I think that this difference between a preference for style versus one for innovation continued until recent times. The innovations of Fazlur Khan, Bertrand Goldberg, and, certainly, Mies van der Rohe cannot find equals in the New York of the 1950s and 1960s. The 1920s and 1930s, however, were different. At that time the style leaders were definitely in New York: Ely Kahn, Raymond Hood, and Van Alen have no equals, with the possible exception of Holabird in Chicago. (Frank Lloyd Wright was not building in Chicago then.)

The importance of Jenney, Sullivan, Root, and Burnham and Company in the late 19th and early 20th centuries is obvious and even the greatness of Messrs. McKim and White, or Carrère and Hastings does not seem to equal the Chicago architectural innovators of that period.

The texture of New York was then and remains to this day a deeper and richer one, layered by hundreds of surprises by mostly anonymous builders spanning three centuries. It is this that ultimately makes the difference between the physical nature of the two cities, and it is the residue of time that enriches New York and gives it the visual edge.

Amy R. Hecker
Executive Director
Landmarks Preservation Council of Illinois

Achieving preservation goals in New York and Chicago proceeds in a one-step-forward-two-steps-back pattern. Although this motion is similar in both cities, the visual character of Chicago's Loop has changed less than has that of downtown Manhattan. Only in the last five to ten years has preservation had a major influence in development decisions. This is due to a number of factors.

Both cities and their respective states have passed a variety of laws which protect landmarks with tools ranging from easements to tax incentives to zoning. Each city has public and private sector advocates who put these tools to work. The tools and their implementation result in preservation success or failure.

New York's landmarks commission has a strong and sophisticated staff, an aggressive program, a working though sometimes difficult relationship with other city departments, and high visibility; Chicago's designation program is weaker. Compared to Chicago's press, New York's has always been a stronger and more articulate voice in favor of preservation. The preservation of important landmarks and areas is gradually becoming a working part of planning in Chicago and New York. Although the public's awareness of historic buildings is increasing, there continues to be opposition from property owners and some special interest groups.

In summary, the abilities of both cities to preserve their historic architecture are improving. But both need more visible public sector commitment, increased educational efforts, and more sophisticated private sector development approaches.

John Hejduk
Architect, New York

The connection that I see between Chicago and New York is the Berlin Connection (that is to say, the connection through Berlin). Berlin serves as the elbow joint/point/connector, Chicago is the hand, and I suppose New York to be the shoulder. It may also be possible to switch the positions of Berlin and New York. All three cities have in common the way they treat steel and their relationship to water. Berlin chooses literally to expose its steel, it shows the rivets, the bolts, and the welds; New York chooses to hide its steel (rather completely) under kinds of veiling. I think somehow that Chicago argues both positions in that it hides and exposes. As for the water …New York, again, hides its water, Chicago gives its water full exposure, and Berlin is the one that both hides and exposes.

The fact that the Berlin/Chicago architect Mies van der Rohe was also to build in New York never ceases to amaze me.

Sarah Bradford Landau
New York University

Like other humanistic disciplines, architectural history is subject to revision. Growth of the field, the detachment of time, and fresh discoveries contribute to reassessment, a situation now affecting late 19th- and early 20th-century American architecture in general and New York and Chicago architecture in particular. A dramatic and long overdue reassessment of the relationship and relative importance of the architecture of the two cities is beginning to crystallize. Reevaluation has been virtually impossible until now. Although aspects of Chicago's architecture have been studied with considerable care and thoroughness — chiefly, the skyscrapers and the work of Frank Lloyd Wright — until relatively recently, New York architecture had been largely neglected by scholars.

Fortunately, the balance is fast being redressed. Indeed, the finest researchers of Chicago architecture are among those now focusing on unstudied and inadequately studied New York material. Regarding New York, a process of discovery that began some years ago with the investigations of Winston Weisman and a few others has been recently rekindled by attention to the production of Hunt, Post, McKim, Mead and White, Flagg, Cass Gilbert, and less well known New York architects, and by the study of specific New York building types. At last, those New York monuments formerly disparaged as ostentatious, lacking in structural "rationalism," and stylistically and technologically "unprogressive" are being given their due. These buildings are now being recognized as the source of significant design schemes and structural innovations previously considered exclusive to Chicago. And their various and elegant design, humanly scaled ornament, and stylistic dialogue with the past are understood as positive characteristics. The time cannot be long before New York's skyscrapers, apartment houses, and town houses figure as significantly in the annals of architecture as Chicago's famed commercial buildings and suburban houses.

Gerald R. Larson
School of Architecture and Interior Design
College of Design, Architecture, Art & Planning
University of Cincinnati

The architectural interactions between New York and Chicago during the past 100 years have been more complementary than past histories will admit. The old cliche of Chicago's technical functionalism competing against New York's lyrical formalism does not represent the truth when one examines the majority of the architecture of the two cities. A close look shows that the only significant departure occurred during the 1880s, when Chicago's architects responded to the nationalism rampant in the late 19th century that paralleled the westward growth of the U.S. by searching for a national style and, thereby, briefly equalled the influence of New York's architects.

Beyond this brief period, one finds the architecture of the two cities paralleling each other whether it is Eclectic (1891-1924), Art Deco (1925-33), Art Moderne (1933-45), International (1945-present), or Post-International. From 1891 to the present, architects of both cities fluctuated between the poles of historicism and modernism, taking their cues from European trends.

For me, the essence of this interaction has been this awareness of European trends, naturally initiated by New York due to its proximity and *disseminated* by its national magazines. Except for the unique but short-lived phenomena of Chicago's 1880s commercial style and the ensuing Prairie School, the great bulk of Chicago's architecture has followed New York's response to European developments. The trend of Chicago (and, indeed, the rest of the country) following New York initiatives may well continue in the future, until Chicago expands its atmosphere of ideas, individuals, and institutions similar to that of the late 19th century which enabled the city's architecture to flourish and inspire.

Richard Meier
Architect, New York

There is no question in my mind that, of any two cities on this continent, none could compare with Chicago and New York in terms of their architectural impact. Yet, each needs the other to make an interactive comparison work. One could not substitute Philadelphia, Boston, or Washington in the equation. Both Chicago and New York have had, historically, a consistently high level of architecture. Over the years New York has been considered the great cultural and artistic center of America, with architecture as a strong part of its vibrant cultural life. The recent intensity of cultural activity on the architecture of Chicago through museum exhibitions, publications, lectures, and tours all suggest the creation of a cultural scene in Chicago that is comparable to that in New York. This keen awareness of architecture as part of cultural life in Chicago and New York, more than anywhere else in America, links both cities and helps in the interaction, with New York architects visiting and working in Chicago and Chicago architects doing the same in New York. Conditions were similar in both cities, historically, in that the grid concept was respected by architects, more or less. I find some recent buildings in both cities very disturbing as architects have disregarded the urban grid. I hope this will recede in frequency, as have sliver buildings in New York.

James Stewart Polshek
Architect, New York

In a true interaction, lines of force must flow in both directions. With respect to Chicago and New York, and their architectural influences upon one another, this has surely been the case. As Chicago developed in the early part of this century, its architecture overtly expressed, in a most Midwestern manner, the rationalism and pragmatism that fueled its mercantile growth. New York, with its immigrant populations and their consequent social pretensions, disguised its passion for economic expansion behind classically romantic facades covered with borrowed rather than invented decoration.

The Chicago/New York interactions that I have identified, however, are paradoxical. The first influences flowed from the Midwest to the East. This interaction involved Chicago's Mies van der Rohe, as interpreted by Gordon Bunshaft of New York's Skidmore, Owings and Merrill and expressed in the following six buildings: Lever House, Manufacturers Hanover Trust, Pepsi-Cola, Union Carbide, Chase Manhattan Bank, and Marine Midland. This Chicago exportation continued through the sixties. After that, things began to change. The earlier positions of the two cities ceased to be so clearly drawn. One of the first chinks in the heretofore impenetrable Miesian armor was Walter Netsch's romantic geometric excursions at the Chicago Circle campus of the University of Illinois. This "new freedom" has now found its way to New York in the guise of Raul DeArmas's recently completed Park Avenue Plaza and Diane Legge Lohan's office tower at 875 Third Avenue. Finally, Helmut Jahn has brought New York's American Renaissance back to Chicago (and Houston), and the circle, albeit terribly deformed, has been completed.

John Portman
Architect, Atlanta

Anything in architecture that can be described as distinctively American owes much of its development to the interaction between Chicago and New York. What has occurred between them is truly interaction, for each has influenced the other and not simply borrowed wholesale. Chicago is a relatively new city, brash, always looking to the future with the confidence that comes of youth and hard muscle. New York is older. Its confidence rests on experience and shrewdness, and its faith is in finesse, while its preoccupation is the need to confront the present.

In broad terms, the differences can be seen in architecture. Chicago's style is bold, willing to break sharply with the past and to show in its designs the technological innovation that makes such departures possible. Chicago's contributions to the development of the skyscraper are the purest expression of this attitude and style. New York, however, has not been a passive borrower of ideas in this interaction. Ideas go into the creative caldron of New York and emerge so changed as to represent original contributions in themselves. New York's architectural innovations have found their way to Chicago as part of a great circular interchange of ideas.

Needless to say, this interaction has been a major influence in shaping American cities and in forming the way architects and the public perceive architecture in the 20th century.

Frank Sanchis
Director of Preservation
New York City Landmarks Preservation Commission

As an historic preservationist, I can't help but speculate as to why organized preservation is so much more developed in New York than in Chicago. I believe that (politics aside), whatever strides have been made in any given area stem directly from the level of involvement of the local citizenry. Therefore, New Yorkers must be more interested in preservation than Chicagoans. Why is that? Perhaps New Yorkers are more involved simply because the city has a longer history than Chicago and contains late 18th- and early 19th-century buildings that satisfy those old-fashioned historical expectations (e.g., "George Washington slept here") that are the foundation of American preservation. If this is the case, then we can look forward to rapidly expanding interest in Chicago as the American public in general (not just preservationists and architectural historians) becomes more aware of the value of late 19th- and early 20th-century buildings, in which Chicago abounds. Having observed that tract housing developers are increasingly forsaking the Colonial and turning to the Victorian for their stylistic inspiration, this moment is obviously just around the corner.

Robert A. M. Stern
Architect, New York

It is a truism, but one worth repeating, that the most characteristic concern of Chicago architects has been with buildings as facts, with designs that constitute what the critic Montgomery Schuyler would have described as "the thing itself." On the other hand, and also a truism, it has been claimed that New York architects have been preoccupied with the transformation of buildings into lithic dreams, three-dimensional poems largely unfettered by circumstance. So be it. Yet, while both attitudes can result in convincing architecture, imbued with the history and character of its particular place, the thing itself, no matter how redolent with integrity, fails to compel us, or at least me, as much as the dream rendered visible. To know what we are is not enough; to envisage what we could be, what we would like to be, is the essence of great art, architectural and otherwise.

Mercifully, functionalism's stronghold on Chicago's commercial architecture has not been total; Sullivan, Burnham, and the Holabird firm in the 1920s brought poetic passion to the demands for "realism" imposed by circumstance. Their work makes it clear that one can build in Chicago, and exemplify Chicago, while going beyond functional and structural determinism. Ironically, two of Chicago's most lyric commercial buildings were designed in the East: the

Marshall Field Warehouse by H. H. Richardson and the Chicago Tribune Tower by Hood and Howells.

To my mind, the great Chicago architects were the ones who were quick to comprehend the differences between tall buildings — high-rises in current parlance — and skyscrapers, between buildings that are merely exceptionally vertical and those that are capable of exhibiting their height with pride and power. True skyscrapers are complex compositions, rising inviolable above the mass of everyday urbanism, yet not contradicting it; tall buildings that combine the urbanism of the street grid with the symbolic individualism of independent form; tall buildings that rise to the level of icons.

Sadly, today, as in the past, nearly all of the ambitious commercial work in Chicago is limited to the factual or the farcical or both. Shrill technicolor essays in the Loop and incoherent masses along North Michigan Avenue neither honor the urban grid nor achieve the iconic clarity of the towers of Sullivan's dreams or Holabird's reality.

Disappointing though the recent work may be, there is at least solace in some of Chicago's suburbs where virtually no trace of architecture solely for building's sake can be found. Generations of Chicago house architects — Maher, Van Doren Shaw, Adler — rubbing shoulders with reinforcements from the East — Harrie T. Lindeberg and Charles Platt — have demonstrated that the architectural task should never be confined to the self-referential, formal problem; their work resonates with psychological nuance expressed through reference to the past.

Stanley Tigerman
Architect, Chicago

The New York-Chicago architectural linkages are many and work in both directions; from the ambulance chasing post-1871 fire travels of P. B. Wight through Henry Ives Cobb's work for Lake Forest Presbyterians to Paul Schweikher's stewardship of Yale's Department of Architecture, to name only a few. Curiously, Chicago architects have sustained the unfortunate mantle of building without an abundance of intellectual support systems while New Yorkers are represented as conceptual intellectuals, unconcerned about the practical matter of building. As the 1980s unfold, nothing could be further from the truth. Consider (a) Charles Gwathmey, a pragmatic, non-intellectual New York architect if there ever was one; (b) Thomas Hall Beeby, an architect whose scholarship is firmly rooted in intrinsically American culture; (c) an Eastern architect like Robert Venturi whose Franklin Square working drawings are solidly pragmatic while; and (d) Mies van der Rohe's 860 Lake Shore Drive working drawings, which are as raggedly generalized as imaginable.

While New York's architecture honestly represents its ethnic diverse anarchy and Chicago's architecture represents its fundamental Protestant work ethic, the Postmodern era has somewhat blurred those distinctions as American pluralism is given form through the several strains of the architecture of our time.

Catalogue

The drawings, models, and other objects included in this exhibition were chosen by Mosette Glaser Broderick, Carol Herselle Krinsky, David Van Zanten, and John Zukowsky. The exhibition is intended to highlight interactions between Chicago and New York, as well as to illustrate the range of architectural treasures in the collections of The New-York Historical Society and The Art Institute of Chicago, the cosponsors of this project. Although selected items were borrowed from several private lenders, principally architectural firms, most of the objects on display are from these two institutions. Thus, the types of objects exhibited represent the institutional and departmental collection policies of the primary repositories.

Founded in 1804, The New-York Historical Society acquired its first architectural drawings in the late 1880s. Today the architectural collections in the Print Room number approximately 140,000 drawings, chiefly from the 1840s to 1930s, plus correspondence, financial ledgers, scrapbooks, and photographs from architects of local, national, and international repute. Although The Art Institute of Chicago was founded in 1879, it was not until 1981 that a Department of Architecture was established. The curatorial department has as its base over 40,000 drawings for Chicago area projects from the mid-19th century through the present which have been collected by the Art Institute's Burnham Library of Architecture since 1919. The library continues to collect related manuscript and photographic material. These two institutional collections, then, reflect their own priorities and policies, but they also solidly represent a full spectrum of New York and Chicago architectural history.

Dimensions are listed in centimeters, height preceding width. Objects are generally listed chronologically. An asterisk (*) denotes that an item will be on exhibit in Chicago and New York only.

I. Elementary Interactions: Chicagoans with New York Projects, New Yorkers in Chicago

1. Peter Bonnett Wight, Architect. Decoration for Dome, Williamsburgh Savings Bank, 175 Broadway, Brooklyn, N.Y., 1873. Pencil and gouache on paper, 53.7 × 54.3. The Art Institute of Chicago, Gift of Peter Bonnett Wight, 1919.

2. Renwick and Sands, Architects. Transverse Section of Second Presbyterian Church, 1936 South Michigan Avenue, Chicago, 1874. Ink on linen working drawing, 59 × 60. The Art Institute of Chicago, Gift of Earl H. Reed and George Eich, 1954.

3. McKim, Mead and White, Architects. Burton Place Elevation of the Mrs. Robert Patterson House, 20 East Burton Place, Chicago, c. 1900. Ink and colored ink on linen, 65 × 92.7. The McKim, Mead and White Collection, The New-York Historical Society.

2

4

5

4. D. H. Burnham and Co., Architects. Perspective Rendering of the Flatiron Building, New York, 1902, delineated by Jules Guérin. Charcoal and ink wash on underpainted linen, 80 × 50.8. The Art Institute of Chicago, Restricted gift of the Thomas J. and Mary E. Eyerman Foundation, 1983.

*5. Helmut Jahn of Murphy/Jahn, Architects. Park Avenue Tower, New York, 1983. Pencil and colored pencil on paper, 228.6 × 62.9. Lent by Helmut Jahn of Murphy/Jahn, Architects.

II. The City Planned

6. William Bridges, surveyor, and Peter Maverick, engraver. Map of the City of New York…, 1811. Colored engraving, approximately 81 × 240. The New-York Historical Society.

*7. C. Bachman, del., Sarony and Major, lith., and John Bachmann, pub. View of New York South from Union Square, 1849. Colored lithograph, approximately 62 × 78. The New-York Historical Society.

8. John Butler Snook, Architect. Vanderbilt Avenue Elevation of Grand Central Station, New York, 1869 (now demolished). Ink and wash on paper, approximately 54.5 × 231. The John B. Snook Collection, The New-York Historical Society.

9. C. L. Cooke, Civil Engineer. Plan of Arch and Truss, Gilbert Elevated Railway, New York, c. 1870. Ink and watercolor on paper, approximately 88 × 102. The New-York Historical Society.

10. Rufus H. Gilbert. Inventor's Model of the First Elevated Railroad, New York, c. 1870. Metalwork on wood base. The New-York Historical Society.

8

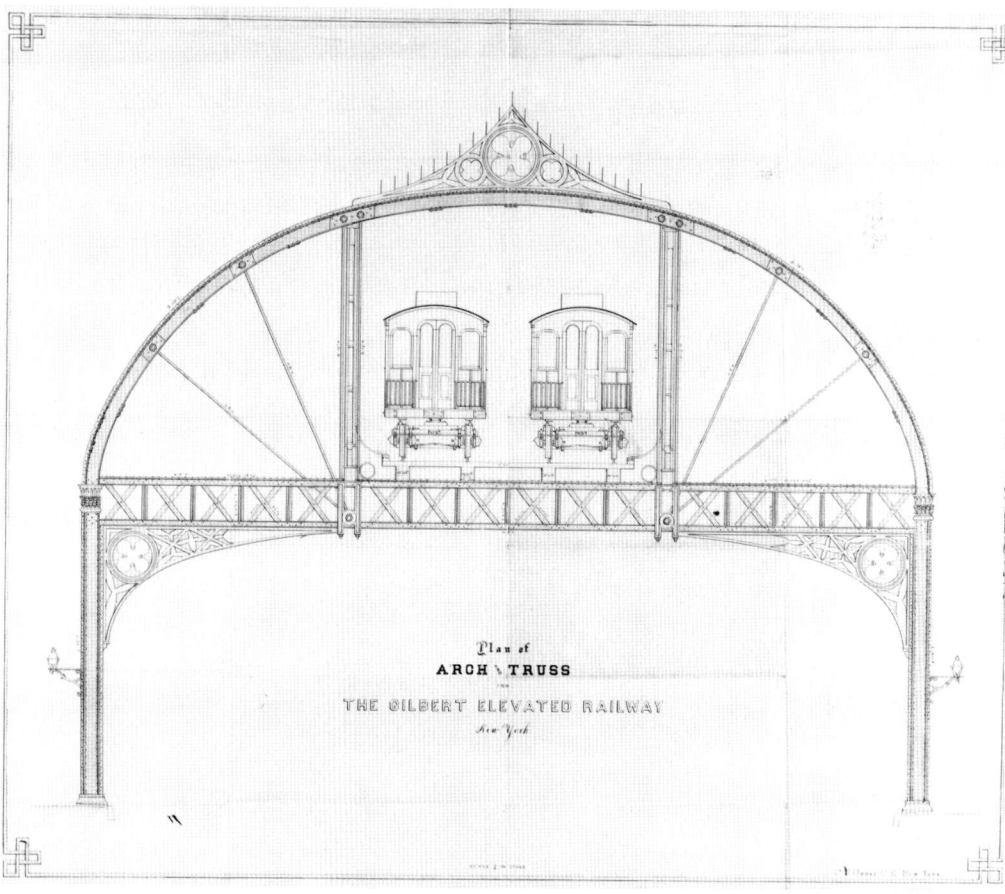

9

11. Daniel H. Burnham and Edward H. Bennett. The Business Center of the City..., c. 1908. Pencil, ink, and wash on paper, 171 × 89.5. Published as Plate 129 in *The Plan of Chicago*, 1909. On permanent loan from the City of Chicago to The Art Institute of Chicago.

12. Daniel H. Burnham and Edward H. Bennett. Chicago. Railway Station Scheme West of the River..., delineated by Jules Guérin, 1908. Pencil and watercolor on paper, 88 × 198. Published as Plate 122 in *The Plan of Chicago*, 1909. On permanent loan from the City of Chicago to The Art Institute of Chicago. (see plate 1)

13. McKim, Mead and White, Architects. Plan of Proposed Fountain and Pavement, 15th Street and 9th Avenue, Brooklyn, 1909. Ink on linen, 61 × 75. The McKim, Mead and White Collection, The New-York Historical Society.

14. Holabird and Root, with Hood, Godley, and Fouilhoux, and Voorhees, Gmelin and Walker, Architects. Plan of Proposed Illinois Central Air Rights Project: Terminal Park, Chicago, c. 1928. Pencil and wash on tracing paper, approximately 64 × 50. The Art Institute of Chicago, Gift of Carol Herselle Krinsky, 1980.

III. Suburban Forms

15 Alexander Jackson Davis, Architect. J. W. Orr, engraver. Eyrie, Eagle Rock, Llewellyn Park, New Jersey, c. 1870. Watercolor and pencil on printed paper, 30.5 × 24. The Alexander J. Davis Collection, The New-York Historical Society.

16. Charles Woodruff, del. Map of Prospect Park, with annotation by McKim, Mead and White, c. 1888-89. Lithograph, ink, and pencil on paper, 40.8 × 61. The McKim, Mead and White Collection, The New-York Historical Society.

17. George Mann Niedecken of Niedecken Walbridge Co. Designs for Hall Chairs, the Avery Coonley House, 281 Bloomingbank Road, Riverside, Illinois, c. 1908. Pencil on paper, 26.5 × 13.5, and ink and watercolor on paper, 24.8 × 15. The Art Institute of Chicago, Department of Architecture Purchase, 1982.

18. Frank Lloyd Wright, Architect. Window from the Avery Coonley House, Riverside, Illinois, 1908. Leaded glass, 111.5 × 52. The Art Institute of Chicago, Gift of Mr. and Mrs. James Howlett, 1973.

19. Tallmadge and Watson, Architects. West Elevation of the Dale Bumstead House, 504 North East Avenue, Oak Park, Illinois, c. 1909. Ink and colored ink on linen, 48 × 74.5. The Art Institute of Chicago, Gift of Emma Watson Estate, 1961.

20. Walter Burley Griffin, Architect. Proposed Ridge Quadrangles, Evanston, Illinois, c. 1910. Ink on linen, 53 × 70.8. The Art Institute of Chicago, Gift of Marion Mahony Griffin, 1949.

IV. Townhouses and Urban Villas

21. Calvin Pollard, Architect. Elevation of an Unidentified Brownstone, New York, c. 1855. Ink and watercolor on paper, 61 × 43.2. The Calvin Pollard Collection, The New-York Historical Society.

22a., 22b. Griffith Thomas, Architect. Second Floor Plan and Madison Avenue Elevation of a Two-Family Townhouse, New York, c. 1890. Ink and watercolor on paper, each 62.4 × 43.2. The New-York Historical Society.

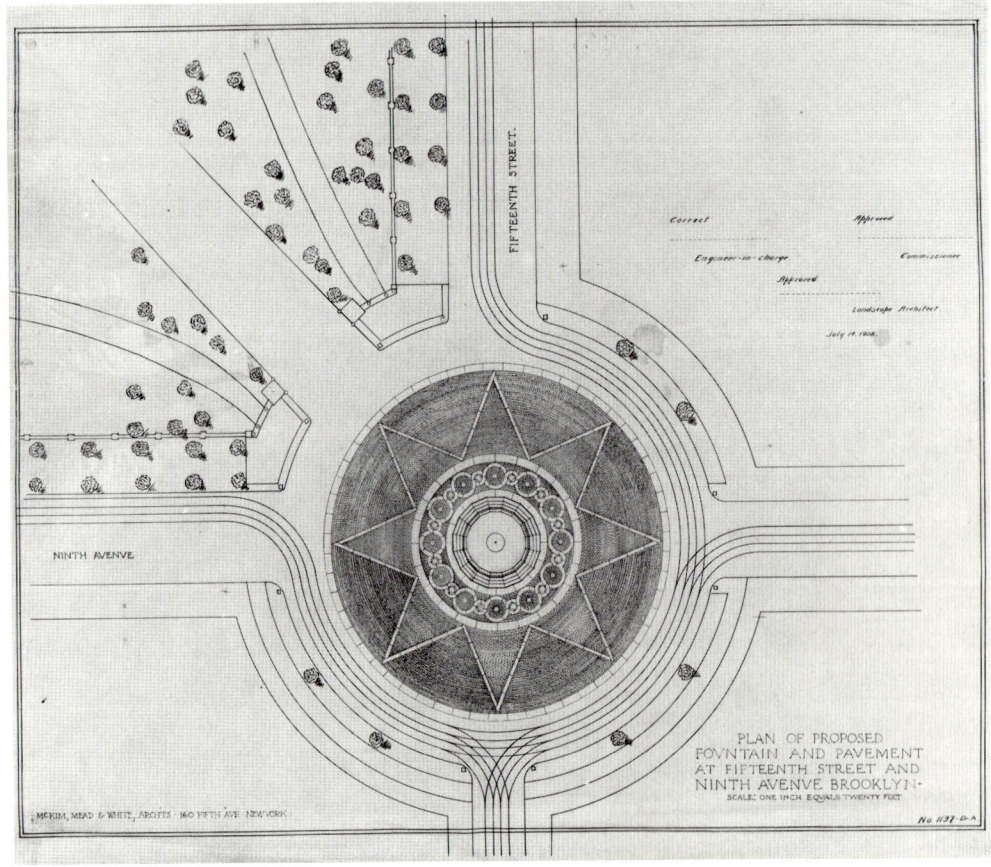

13

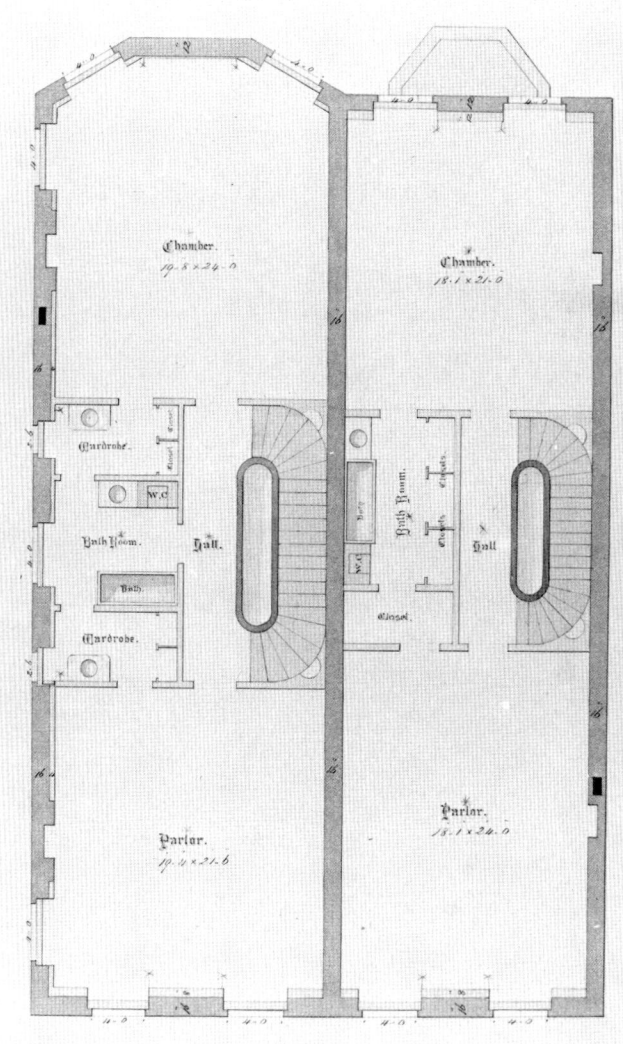

22a

22b

23. Adler and Sullivan, Architects. Double House for Mr. Straus, Chicago, 1883. Ink on paper, approximately 44.5 × 51.8. Published in *Inland Architect* (June 1884). The Art Institute of Chicago, Gift of Richard Nickel, 1957.

24. John Wellborn Root of Burnham and Root, Architects. Perspective Rendering of the William J. Goudy House, Chicago, c. 1889 (now demolished). Pencil and wash on paper, 53 × 45.5. The Art Institute of Chicago, Gift of Dr. and Mrs. Stanton Fletcher.

23

24

25. George B. Post, Architect. Cornelius Vanderbilt House, 1 West 57th Street, 1879-82, enlarged 1892 (now demolished). Perspective rendering for enlargement by J. Vincent. Charcoal on paper, approximately 67 × 87. The George B. Post Collection, The New-York Historical Society.

26. George B. Post, Architect. Longitudinal Section Looking West for the Enlargement of the Cornelius Vanderbilt House, New York, 1892. Pencil and wash on paper, 77.5 × 134.5. The George B. Post Collection, The New-York Historical Society.

27. McKim, Mead and White, Architects. Elevation of the Bryan Lathrop House, 120 East Bellevue Place, Chicago, 1892. Ink and colored ink on linen, 62 × 67. The Art Institute of Chicago, Gift of Holabird and Root, 1973.

28. McKim, Mead and White, Architects. Plan and Elevations for the Vestibule, Bryan Lathrop House, Chicago, c. 1892. Ink and watercolor on linen, 38.5 × 40.5. The Art Institute of Chicago, Gift of Holabird and Root, 1973.

29. Holabird and Roche, Architects. Book Cases for Bryan Lathrop House, Chicago, 1898. Ink and colored ink on linen, 52.7 × 66. The Art Institute of Chicago, Gift of Holabird and Root, 1973.

30. Richard E. Schmidt, Architect. Burton Street Elevation of the Albert F. Madlener House, 4 West Burton Place, Chicago, 1902. Ink and colored ink on linen, 52.5 × 76. The Art Institute of Chicago, Gift of Schmidt, Garden and Erikson, 1977.

25

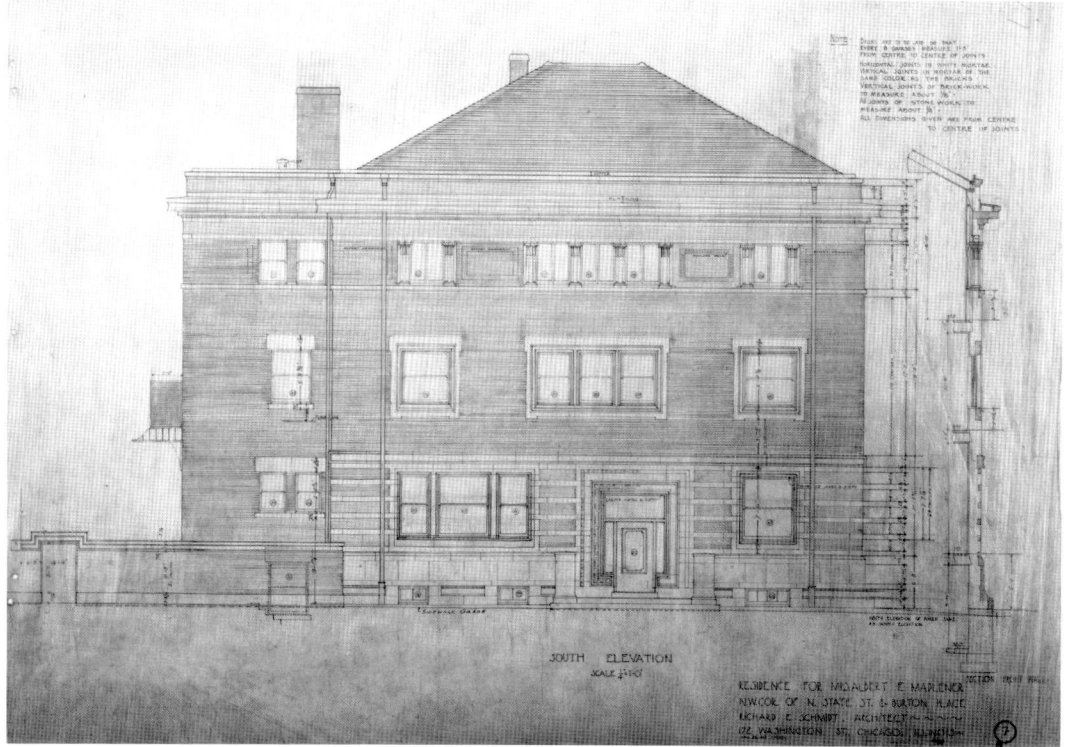

30

V. Apartment Houses

31. James E. Ware, Architect. The Osborne Apartments, 205 West 57th Street, New York, 1885, with later additions. Photoprint, 43.5 × 34.3. The New-York Historical Society.

32. Clinton and Russell, Architects. The Apthorp Apartments, 2207 Broadway, New York, 1908. Photoprint of perspective rendering by E. Eldon Deane, c. 1906, 52 × 71.5. The New-York Historical Society.

33. Dubin and Eisenberg, Architects. Perspective Rendering of the Boulevard Apartments, Chicago, c. 1920, by Charles Morgan. Pencil, chalk, and watercolor on paper, mounted on board, approximately 74 × 91. The Art Institute of Chicago, Gift of Dubin, Dubin and Moutoussamy, the successor firm to Dubin and Eisenberg, 1983.

34. Benjamin Leo Steif. Sketches of the Savoy Plaza Hotel and the Insurance Center, New York, c. 1927-28. Pencil on note paper, 26.8 × 20.5. The Art Institute of Chicago, Gift of Mrs. Irving Stein, Sr., 1980.

35. McNally and Quinn, Architects, with Rosario Candela, Associate Architect. Sketch Elevation of 1500 Lake Shore Drive, Chicago, c. 1928, delineated by George Hossack. Ink and pencil on tracing paper, approximately 66 × 52. The Art Institute of Chicago, Gift of James Edwin Quinn, 1980.

36. McNally and Quinn, Architects, with Rosario Candela, Associate Architect. Full-Size Details of Urns and Finials, 1500 Lake Shore Drive, Chicago, 1928, delineated by George Hossack. Pencil on tracing paper, approximately 68 × 105. The Art Institute of Chicago, Gift of James Edwin Quinn, 1980.

32

33

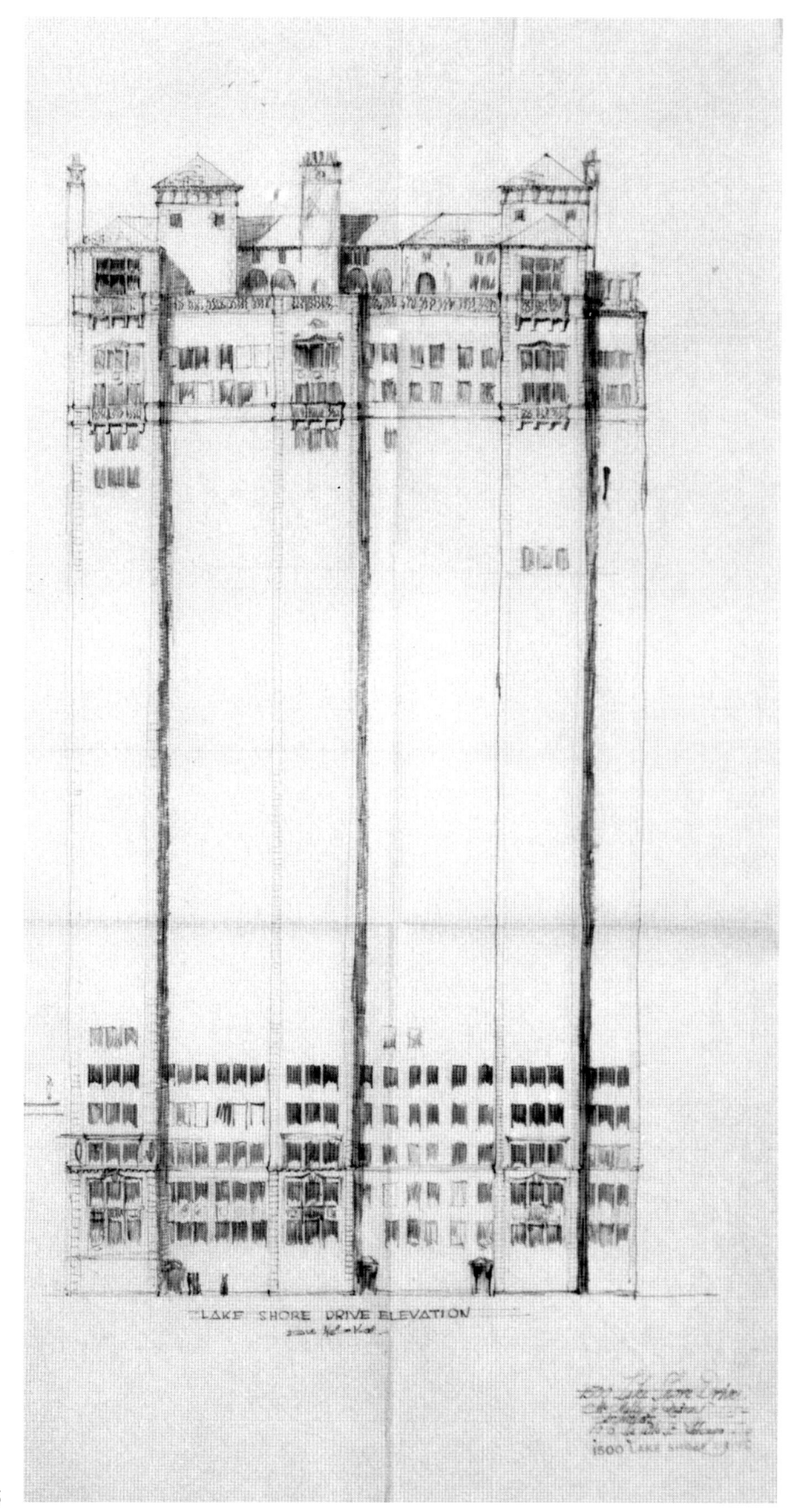

37. Emery Roth, Architect. The San Remo Apartments, 145 Central Park West, New York, 1929-30. Photoprint by Leonard Lubbock, 33.8 × 26.8. The New-York Historical Society.

38. William D. Wilson of The Gruzen Partnership, Architects. Perspective Rendering of the Montana Apartments, 247 West 87th Street, New York, 1983, delineated by Peter Gumbel. Colored pencil and photostat, 61 × 41.9. Lent by the Gruzen Partnership, Architects, Planners.

39. Laurence Booth of Booth Hansen and Associates. Facade Study for 320 North Michigan Avenue, 1981. Pencil and colored pencil on paper, 61 × 45.5. The Art Institute of Chicago, Anonymous gift, 1981.

37

38

VI. Commercial Buildings

40. J. Trench and Co., Architects. Chambers Street Elevation of the A. T. Stewart Store, New York, 1846 (now demolished). Ink and watercolor on paper, 53 × 74. The John B. Snook Collection, The New-York Historical Society.

41. John Butler Snook, Architect. Detail of the Front and Rear Elevations, 184 Fifth Avenue, New York, 1872 (now demolished). Pencil, ink, and watercolor on paper, 45 × 66. The John B. Snook Collection, The New-York Historical Society.

40

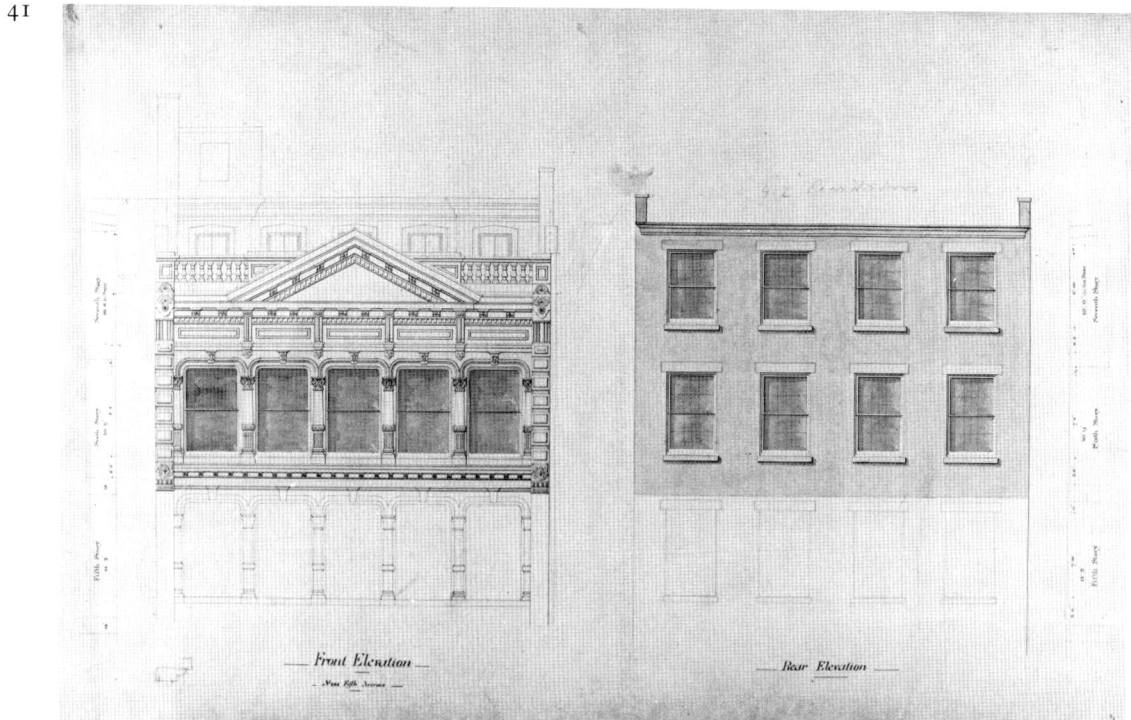

41

42. John Butler Snook, Architect. Part Elevation and Section of the Cast-Iron Facade, 184 Fifth Avenue, 1872 (now demolished). Ink and watercolor on linen, 80 × 58.5. The John B. Snook Collection, The New-York Historical Society.

43. Carter, Drake, and Wight, Architects. Perspective Rendering of the Lenox Building, Chicago, 1872 (now demolished), delineated by John Wellborn Root. Ink and wash on paper, 51.2 × 25. The Art Institute of Chicago, Gift of Peter Bonnett Wight, 1919.

44. Carter, Drake, and Wight, Architects. The Stewart-Bentley Building, Chicago, 1872 (now demolished), delineated by D. H. Burnham. Ink and watercolor on paper, 55.9 × 29. The Art Institute of Chicago, Gift of Peter Bonnett Wight, 1919.

*45. J. J. Fogerty, Publisher. Broadway, View North from Maiden Lane and Cortlandt Street, New York, c. 1880, showing George B. Post's Western Union Building. Colored lithograph, approximately 84 × 109. The New-York Historical Society.

46. Solon Spencer Beman, Architect. Framing Plan and Steel Construction Diagram, The Pullman Building, Chicago, 1884 (now demolished). Ink and colored ink on linen, approximately 66 × 102. The Art Institute of Chicago, Gift of Jeremy Beman, 1974.

47. George B. Post, Architect. Transverse Section of the New York Produce Exchange, c. 1881-85 (now demolished). Ink and watercolor on paper, 95.2 × 106.8. The George B. Post Collection, The New-York Historical Society.

48. Sackett, Wilhelms, and Betzig, Lithographers. Advertising poster for James H. Seymour, showing George B. Post's Produce Exchange, New York, c. 1885. Lithograph, approximately 94 × 106. The New-York Historical Society. (see plate 2)

49. Adler and Sullivan, Architects. Ornamental Details for Auditorium Office Building and Hotel, Chicago, c. 1887. Hectograph print, 54.5 × 83.5. The Art Institute of Chicago, Gift of George Grant Elmslie, 1931.

43

45

47

50. Adler and Sullivan, Architects, with Baumann and Cady, Consulting Architects. Elevation of the Schiller Building, Chicago, 1891 (now demolished). Hectograph print, 100 × 40.5 The Art Institute of Chicago, Gift of Balaban and Katz, 1962.

51. Adler and Sullivan, Architects. Section of Stenciled Frieze from the Chicago Stock Exchange Trading Room, 1894 (now demolished), executed by Healy and Millet. Oil on canvas, 143.7 × 305.4 × 1. The Art Institute of Chicago, Gift of Mr. and Mrs. Arthur D. Dubin, 1971. The Trading Room was reconstructed in 1976-77 at The Art Institute of Chicago; Gift of The Walter B. Heller Foundation through its president, Mrs. Edwin J. DeCosta. (see plate 3)

52. Adler and Sullivan, T-Plate from the Elevator Grills of the Chicago Stock Exchange Building, 1893-94 (now demolished). Stamped copper, 40.7 × 44.2. The Art Institute of Chicago, Gift of Sudler and Co., 1960.

53. George B. Post, Architect. Park Row Elevation of the New York Times Building, 41 Park Row, New York c. 1888-89. Altered in 1905 by Robert Maynicke, Architect. Ink and colored ink on linen, 155 × 89 cm. The George B. Post Collection, The New-York Historical Society.

54. Richard E. Schmidt, Architect. Elevation of the Montgomery Ward Tower, 6 North Michigan Avenue, Chicago, c. 1898 (later altered). Ink on linen, approximately 106 × 48. The Art Institute of Chicago, Gift of Schmidt, Garden and Erikson, 1977.

55. George B. Post, Architect. Perspective Rendering of the New York Stock Exchange Building, 8 Broad Street, New York, 1900. Later addition in 1923 by Trowbridge and Livingston, Architects. Watercolor on paper, delineated by Hughson Hawley (mounted on masonite), 125.5 × 110.7. The George B. Post Collection, The New-York Historical Society. (see plate 4)

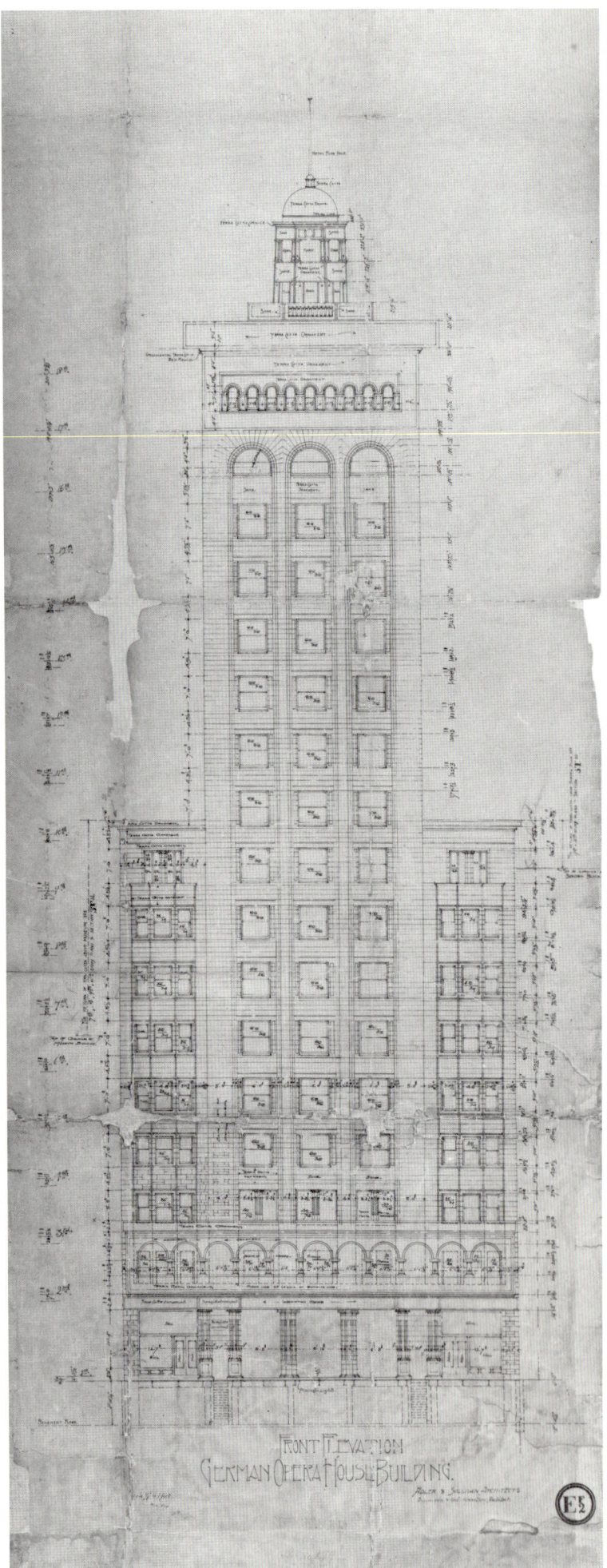

50

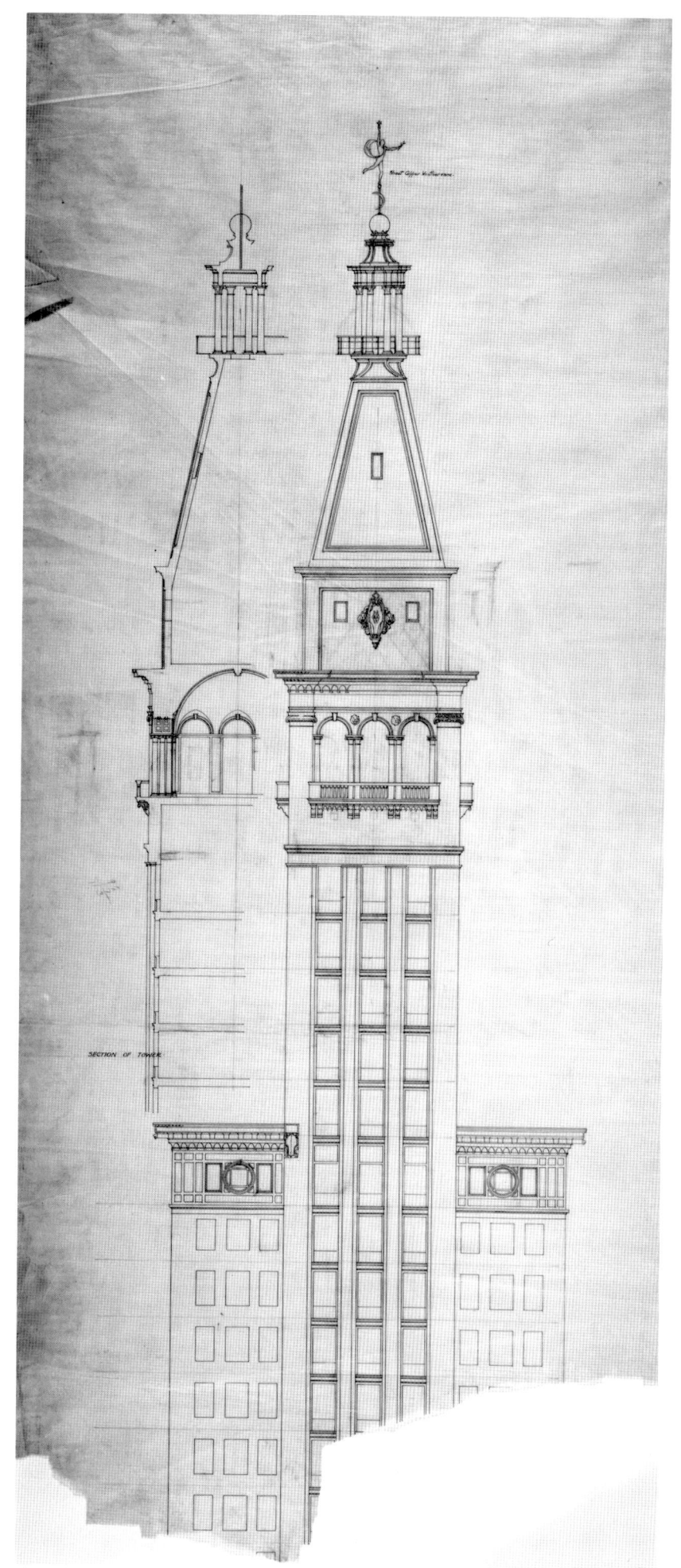

54

VII. Skyscrapers

56. Ernest Flagg, Architect. The Singer Building, New York, 1902 (now demolished). Lithograph of perspective rendering by Hughson Hawley, 183 × 87. The New-York Historical Society.

57. Cass Gilbert, Architect. Four Studies for the Woolworth Building, 233 Broadway, New York, 1910. Pencil, pastel, and watercolor by T. R. Johnson on illustration board, 42 × 19.5, 56.5 × 23.5, 73.7 × 32, and 52.7 × 26.5. The Gilbert Collection, The New-York Historical Society. (see plate 5)

*58. Cass Gilbert, Architect. Copper finial from the Woolworth Building, New York, 1913. 185.4 × 47 × 47. Lent by Kelmscott Gallery, Chicago.

59. Richard Yoshijiro Mine, Architect. Elevation of Competitive Design for the Chicago Tribune Tower, 1922. Ink and wash on paper, 140.3 × 59.7. The Art Institute of Chicago, Gift of Richard Yoshijiro Mine, 1979.

56

59

60. McKim, Mead and White, Architects. Elevation of the Municipal Building, Chambers and Centre Streets, New York, c. 1907. Ink and wash on paper, 187 × 141. The McKim, Mead and White Collection, The New-York Historical Society.

61. Alfred S. Alschuler, Architect. Elevation of the London Guarantee and Accident Company Building (now Stone Container Building), 360 North Michigan Avenue, Chicago, 1922. Ink on linen, 132 × 75. The Art Institute of Chicago, Gift of Friedman, Alschuler and Sincere, 1980.

62. Howells and Hood, Architects. Studies for the Chicago Tribune Tower, Chicago, c. 1923. Photoprints of architectural renderings, each approximately 24 × 15. The Raymond Hood Collection, The New-York Historical Society.

60

VIII. Modern to Postmodern Skyscrapers

63. Skidmore, Owings and Merrill, Architects. First Model for the Inland Steel Building, 30 West Monroe Street, Chicago, c. 1954, preliminary design by Walter A. Netsch. Plexiglass and enameled steel, approximately 28 × 27 × 18. The Art Institute of Chicago, Gift of Walter A. Netsch, 1981.

63

64. Robert A. M. Stern, Architect. Late Entry to the Chicago Tribune Tower Competition, 1980. Airbrushed ink on board, 80 × 50.8. The Art Institute of Chicago, Restricted Gifts of Mr. and Mrs. Thomas J. Eyerman, Mr. and Mrs. David Hilliard, and Mr. and Mrs. Ben Weese, 1983.

65. Helmut Jahn of Murphy/Jahn, Architects. Proposed 425 Lexington Avenue, New York, 1983. Pencil and colored pencil on paper, 228.6 × 106.7. Lent by Helmut Jahn of Murphy/Jahn, Architects.

66. Edward Larrabee Barnes, Architect. Perspective Rendering of the Proposed Equitable Center, New York, 1983. Pencil and colored pencil on paper, 73.7 × 50.3. Lent by the Equitable Life Assurance Society of the U.S.

IX. Celebrating the City

67. Carstensen and Gildemeister, Architects. The Crystal Palace, New York World's Fair, 1853, with the Latting Observatory. Colored engraving, 48.3 × 61.5. The New-York Historical Society.

68. Carstensen and Gildemeister, Architects. The Crystal Palace, New York World's Fair, 1853. Interior view delineated by Charles Parsons, lithographed by Endicott and Co. Colored lithograph, 43 × 60.8. The New-York Historical Society.

67

69. Carstensen and Gildemeister, Architects. Facade Elevation of Proposed New-York Historical Society, 1854. Ink and watercolor on paper, 62 × 46. The New-York Historical Society.

70. John Wellborn Root, Architect. Preliminary Study for Buildings and the Canal at the World's Columbian Exposition, Chicago, c. 1890. Pencil on paper mounted on illustration board, 38.2 × 53.2. The Art Institute of Chicago, Gift of Edwin and Marguerite Fletcher, 1970.

70

71. John Wellborn Root, Architect. Preliminary Design for a Museum of Fine Arts, World's Columbian Exposition, Chicago, c. 1891 (unexecuted), delineated by Paul Lautrup. Watercolor and pencil on paper, 55.5 × 115. The Art Institute of Chicago, Gift of John Wellborn Root, Jr., 1945.

71

72. Augustus Saint-Gaudens, Sculptor. Preliminary Sketch for the Statue of the Republic, 1891. Executed later by Daniel Chester French at the World's Columbian Exposition, Chicago, 1893. Pencil on tracing paper, approximately 20 × 6. The Art Institute of Chicago, Gift of Daniel and Hubert Burnham, 1945.

73. Daniel Chester French, Sculptor. Elevation of Reduced-Scale Copy of the Statue of the Republic, Chicago, 1915. Ink and watercolor on paper, 53.5 × 40.5. The Art Institute of Chicago, Gift of the Benjamin F. Ferguson Monument Fund.

74. Ralph Walker of Voorhees, Gmelin and Walker, Architects. Preliminary Study for Proposed Tower of Water and Light, Century of Progress Exposition, Chicago, c. 1929. Pencil on paper, 61 × 58.3. The Art Institute of Chicago, Architecture Purchase, 1980.

75. Ralph Walker of Voorhees, Gmelin and Walker, Architects. Perspective Rendering of the Final Design for a Proposed Tower of Water and Light, Century of Progress Exposition, Chicago, 1930, delineated by John Wenrich. Pencil and watercolor on illustration board, 68.5 × 47. The Art Institute of Chicago, Gift of Haines Lundberg Waehler in honor of their centennial, 1983. (see plate 6)

76. Chicago Chapter of the American Institute of Architects at Raymond Hood's American Radiator Exhibit, Century of Progress Exposition, Chicago, 1933. Photoprint by Kaufmann-Fabry, 30.5 × 47.2. The Raymond Hood Collection, The New-York Historical Society.

77. Ernest A. Grunsfeld, Jr., Architect. Elevations of the Lumber Industries House, Century of Progress Exposition, Chicago, 1933. Pencil on tracing paper, 59.5 × 94. The Art Institute of Chicago, Gift of Mr. and Mrs. Ernest Grunsfeld III, 1981.

78. George Fred Keck, Architect, with Alexander Archipenko, Glass Muralist. Perspective Study of Proposed Exhibition Booth for the Libbey, Owens, Ford Glass display, New York World's Fair, 1939 (unexecuted). Pencil, ink, and watercolor on illustration board, 38 × 53 cm. The Art Institute of Chicago, Gift of William Keck, 1983.

Photography credits

All photographs are from the collection of the Ryerson and Burnham Libraries of The Art Institute of Chicago, except for the following:

Chicago Architectural Photographing Co., © David R. Phillips, figs. 10, 52, 61, 71
Janet Ginsburg and Nancy Thill, fig. 1
Hedrich-Blessing, Ltd., fig. 69
Wolfgang Hoyt, Esto, fig. 78
Howard N. Kaplan, © HNK Architectural Photography, fig. 25
Robert A. Knudtsen, fig. 28
Courtesy Kohn, Pedersen and Fox, fig. 8
Gregory Murphey, fig. 7
The New-York Historical Society, figs. 13, 15, 19, 40, 42, 57, 63
Richard Nickel, courtesy the Richard Nickel Committee, fig. 2
The Rapp and Rapp Collection, fig. 4
Ezra Stoller, Esto, figs. 5, 27, 49, 50
Bob Thall, figs. 6, 16, 58, pl. 3
Tigerhill Studio, figs. 22, 76, 77